Piano

Classical Piano Anthology 3

18 Original Works
Including pieces by Oginski, Beethoven, Voříšek
and Schubert

Selected and edited by Nils Franke

ED 13440
ISMN 979-0-2201-3275-9
ISBN 978-1-84761-259-5

www.schott-music.com

Mainz • London • Berlin • Madrid • New York • Paris • Prague • Tokyo • Toronto
© 2013 SCHOTT MUSIC Ltd, London • Printed in Germany

Acknowledgements / Remerciements / Danksagung

I am grateful to Mary and David Bowerman whose generous support has enabled the CD to be recorded in the excellent setting of Champs Hill Music Room. A special mention must go to the production team of the CD, Ateş Orga and Ken Blair, for their expertise and contribution to this project.

Je remercie Mary et David Bowerman dont le généreux soutien a permis d'enregistrer le CD dans les excellentes conditions offertes par le Champs Hill Music Room. Il me faut également citer tout particulièrement l'équipe de production du CD, Ateş Orga et Ken Blair, pour leur savoir-faire et leur précieuse contribution à ce projet.

Ich danke Mary und David Bowerman für ihre großzügige Unterstützung, die es ermöglicht hat, die CD im großartigen Ambiente des Champs Hill Music Room aufzunehmen. Ein besonderer Dank geht an das Produktionsteam der CD, Ateş Orga und Ken Blair für ihr Know-how und ihren Beitrag zu diesem Projekt.

Nils Franke

ED 13440
British Library Cataloguing-in-Publication Data.
A catalogue record for this book is available from the British Library
ISMN 979-0-2201-3275-9
ISBN 978-1-84761-259-5

CD recorded in Champs Hill, West Sussex, 8th June 2011, on a Steinway D Concert Grand with Nils Franke, Piano
Producer: Ateş Orga
Editor and Engineer: Ken Blair
Cover image: 'Blick in das Tal von Kreuth' (c. 1810), by Wilhelm von Kobell

French translation: Michaëla Rubi
German translation: Heike Brühl
Music setting and page layout: Darius Heise-Krzyszton, www.notensatzstudio.de

Printed in Germany S&Co.8761

Contents / Sommaire / Inhalt

The Pieces / Les pièces / Die Stücke

Introduction

The present collection of piano pieces is the third volume in a series of four books covering the piano music in the classical period from grades 1-8. It follows on from a format established in the *Romantic Piano Anthologies* Vols.1-4 (ED 12912 to ED 12915).

While anthologies are, inevitably, a personal selection of music they can nevertheless be underpinned by specific selection criteria. In the case of the present series, it has been my intention to include works that are idiomatically written, are indicative of their period and, above all, are useful in the development of pianistic skills for players at this stage of their development.

In the selection of repertoire I have tried to achieve a balance between established teaching pieces, rare works of the period, and between some of the main composers of the era and their lesser-known contemporaries. I hope that this can in some way attempt to reflect the diversity of styles within music from the 1780s to the 1820s.

The repertoire is presented broadly in an order of ascending difficulty, though I hope that the suggested sequence can be seen as a recommendation, rather than a restriction. The music included in this book is aimed at players of Grades 5-6 standard (UK) or intermediate to upper intermediate level (USA), or pianists of five to six years' playing experience (Europe).

The teaching notes are designed to assist students by offering some suggestions on how to approach a particular section within a piece. Also included are suggestions for topics that may need to be considered when playing classical piano music on a modern instrument, as the fortepiano of the late 18th century was of a different construction to the modern piano. The commentary cannot, and is not intended to, replace the collaborative spirit of exploration that teachers and students share in their lessons.

One of the most rewarding aspects of instrumental teaching is watching students become independent learners who make their own decisions and develop their own performance skills. I hope that the *Classical Piano Anthologies* can in some way contribute to this development.

Nils Franke

Introduction

Ce recueil de pièces pour piano constitue le troisième volet d'une collection en quatre volumes consacrés à la musique pour piano de la période classique, du niveau 1 au niveau 8. Du point de vue formel, il se calque sur le format établi dans l'*Anthologie du piano romantique*, volumes 1 à 4 (ED 12912 to ED 12915).

Le fait qu'une anthologie reflète inévitablement des choix personnels n'empêche pas qu'elle puisse être néanmoins sous-tendue par des critères de sélection spécifiques. Concernant la présente collection, j'ai choisi d'inclure des œuvres à l'écriture idiomatique, caractéristiques de leur période et, avant tout, utiles au développement des compétences pianistiques des instrumentistes à ce niveau de leur progression.

Pour ce qui concerne le choix du répertoire, j'ai tenté d'établir un équilibre, à la fois entre des pièces appartenant traditionnellement au répertoire pédagogique et des œuvres rares de cette période, et entre des compositeurs majeurs et leurs contemporains moins célèbres. J'espère que cela permettra, d'une certaine manière, d'illustrer la diversité des styles musicaux des années 1780 à 1820.

Globalement, le répertoire est présenté par ordre croissant de difficulté, mais j'espère que la progression suggérée sera considérée davantage comme une suggestion que comme une contrainte. La musique pro-

posée dans cet ouvrage s'adresse à des musiciens de niveau 5 à 6 standard (RU), intermédiaire à intermédiaire avancé (USA), ou à des pianistes possédant au moins cinq à six ans de pratique instrumentale (Europe).

Les notes pédagogiques ont pour objectif d'aider les élèves en leur suggérant des axes de travail dans l'approche de certains passages spécifiques à l'intérieur des morceaux. Dans la mesure où le pianoforte de la fin du 18e siècle était de facture différente du piano moderne, elles proposent également une réflexion sur les thématiques à aborder lorsque l'on joue de la musique classique sur un instrument moderne. Ces commentaires ne peuvent ni ne prétendent se substituer à l'esprit de collaboration et d'exploration que partagent le maître et l'élève pendant la leçon.

L'un des aspects les plus gratifiants de l'enseignement instrumental est de voir ses élèves devenir indépendants, expérimenter différentes pistes musicales et développer leurs propres dons. J'espère qu'à leur manière, ces *Anthologies du piano classique* pourront contribuer à ce développement.

Nils Franke

Einleitung

Die vorliegende Sammlung mit Klavierstücken ist der dritte Band einer vierbändigen Reihe mit klassischer Klaviermusik für alle Schwierigkeitsgrade. Sie ist genauso aufgebaut wie die *Romantic Piano Anthology* Bd. 1–4 (ED 12912 bis ED 12915).

Eine Anthologie enthält zwar immer eine subjektive Auswahl von Musikstücken, doch können natürlich bestimmte Auswahlkriterien herangezogen werden. Mein Anliegen bei der Zusammenstellung der vorliegenden Reihe war eine Auswahl von Musikstücken, die idiomatisch geschrieben, typisch für ihre Epoche und vor allem im Hinblick auf klavierspielerische Aspekte für Pianisten der jeweiligen Spielstufe nützlich sind.

Bei der Auswahl der Stücke habe ich versucht, ein ausgewogenes Verhältnis zwischen bewährtem Unterrichtsmaterial und selten gespielten klassischen Werken sowie zwischen einigen der wichtigsten Komponisten dieser Epoche und ihren weniger bekannten Zeitgenossen herzustellen. Ich hoffe, dass dies die Stilvielfalt der Musik von den 1780er- bis zu den 1820er-Jahren.

Die Stücke sind weitgehend nach aufsteigendem Schwierigkeitsgrad geordnet, wobei die vorgeschlagene Reihenfolge als Empfehlung und nicht als Einschränkung aufgefasst werden sollte. Die Stücke in diesem Buch richten sich an Spieler der Stufe 5–6 (Großbritannien), Mittelstufe bis obere Mittelstufe (USA) bzw. Pianisten mit mindestens fünf bis sechs Jahren Spielpraxis (Europa).

Die Spielhinweise sollen die Schüler mit Hilfe von Vorschlägen für bestimmte Passagen an das jeweilige Stück heranführen. Darüber hinaus enthält die Anthologie Vorschläge, die eventuell berücksichtigt werden müssen, wenn man klassische Klaviermusik auf einem modernen Instrument spielt, da sich das Pianoforte des späten 18. Jahrhunderts vom modernen Klavier unterschied. Die Anmerkungen können und sollen jedoch nicht die gemeinsame Beschäftigung von Lehrern und Schülern mit dem Stück im Unterricht ersetzen.

Eine der schönsten Belohnungen beim Unterrichten eines Instruments ist, zu beobachten, wie die Schüler unabhängig werden, eigene Entscheidungen treffen und ihren eigenen Spielstil entwickeln. Ich hoffe, dass die Bände der *Classical Piano Anthology* einen Betrag zu dieser Entwicklung leisten können.

Nils Franke

1. Allegretto

(after Hob. XXVIII:8 [Sinfonia])

Joseph Haydn
(1732 – 1809)

Allegretto
(♩. = 76)

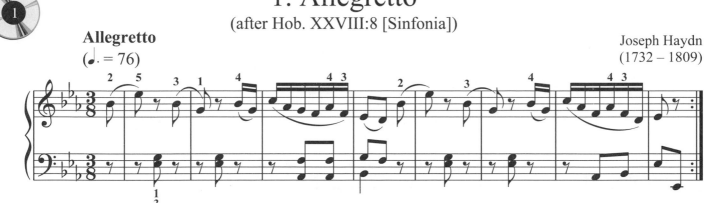

2. Allegretto

(after Hob. XXVIII:8 [Aria])

Joseph Haydn
(1732 – 1809)

Allegretto
(♩. = 52)

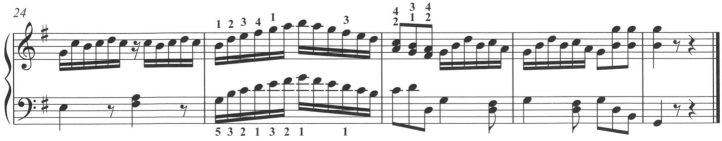

3. Deutscher Tanz

KV 509 No. 3

Wolfgang Amadeus Mozart
(1756 – 1791)

Allegretto
(♩. = 66–72)

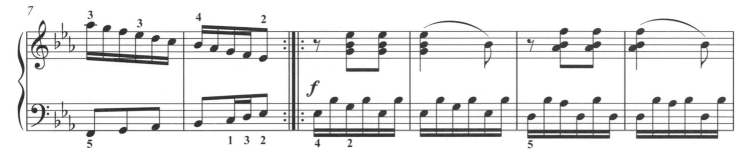

D. C. (Maggiore)
al Fine senza rip.

4. Allegro moderato

[in F]

Leopold Mozart
(1719 – 1787)

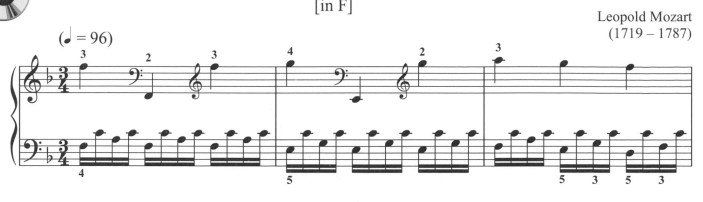

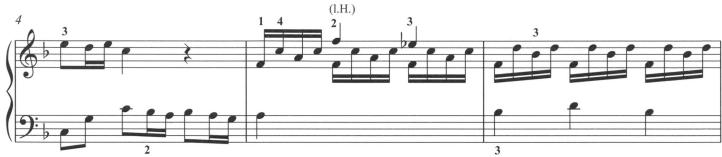

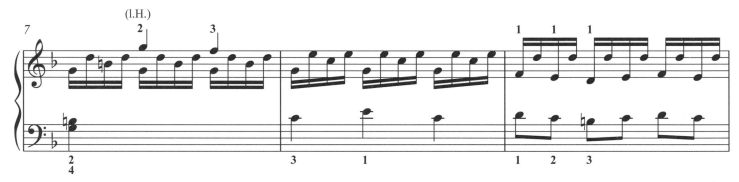

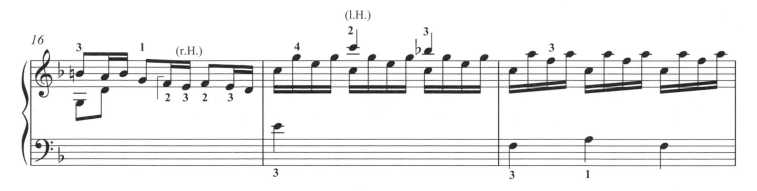

5. Walzer

J. App. II/81

Carl Maria von Weber
(1786 – 1826)

Fine

D. C. al Fine

6. Polonaise

[in F]

Michał Kleofas Ogiński
(1765 – 1833)

Fine

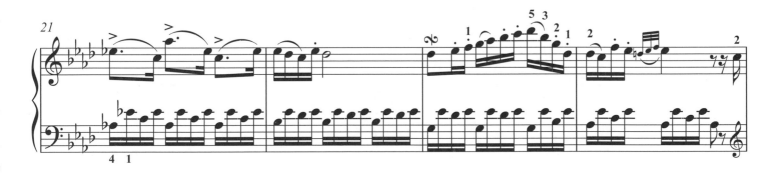

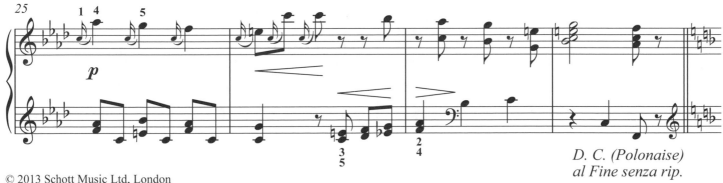

D. C. (Polonaise)
al Fine senza rip.

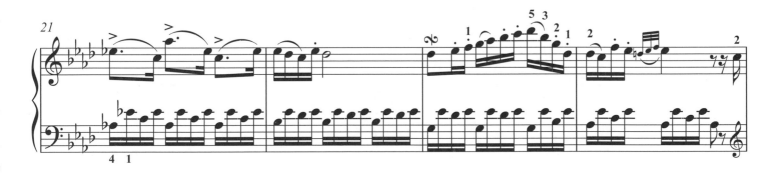

7. Walzer
WoO84

Ludvig van Beethoven
(1770 – 1827)

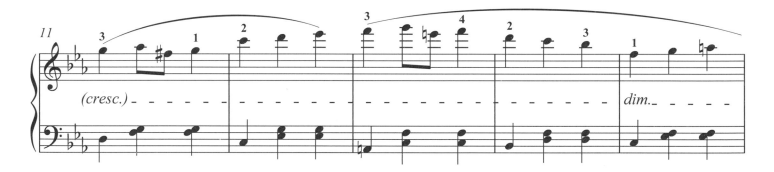

Fine

Trio

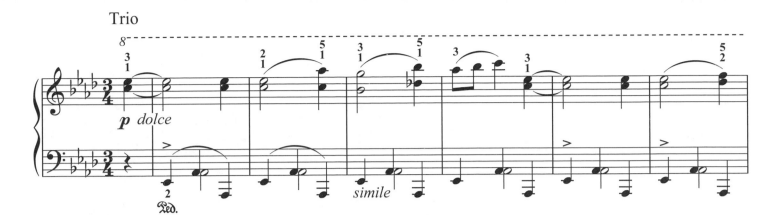

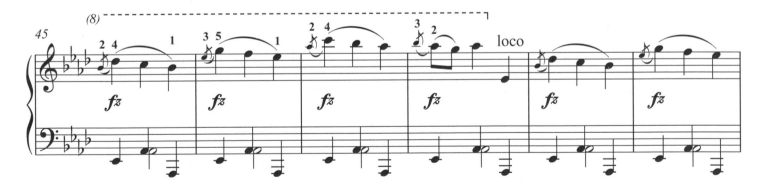

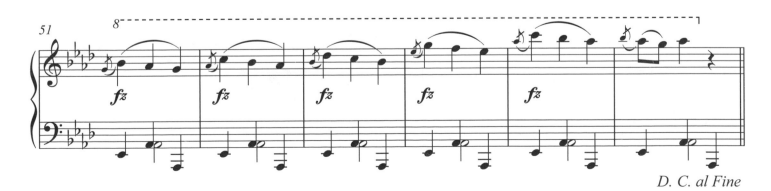

D. C. al Fine

8. Allegro con brio

No. 45, *from* Pianoforte method

Johann Nepomuk Hummel
(1778 – 1837)

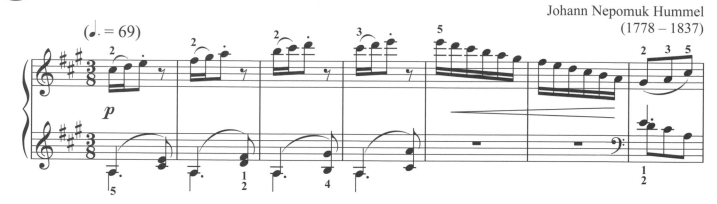

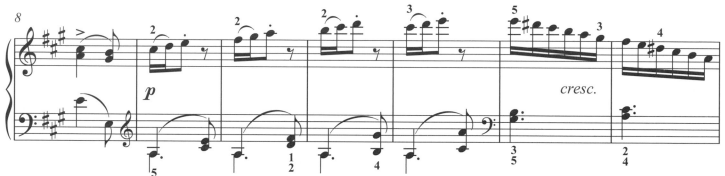

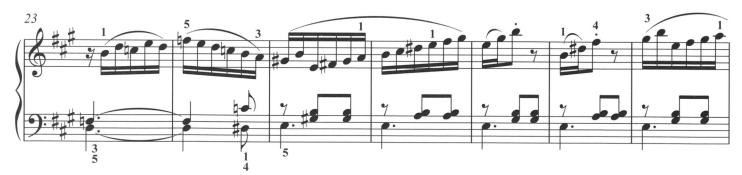

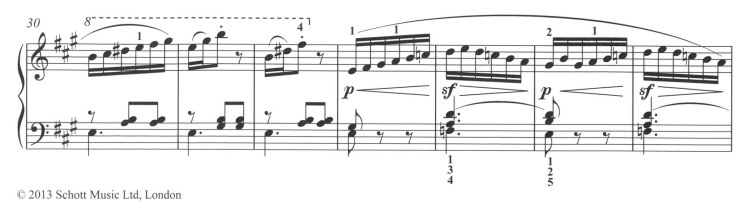

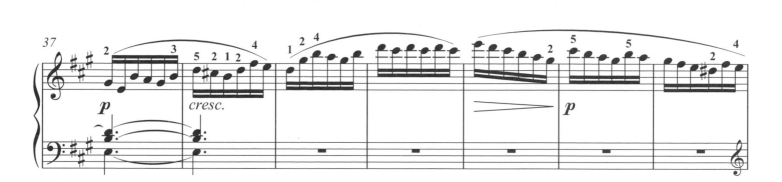

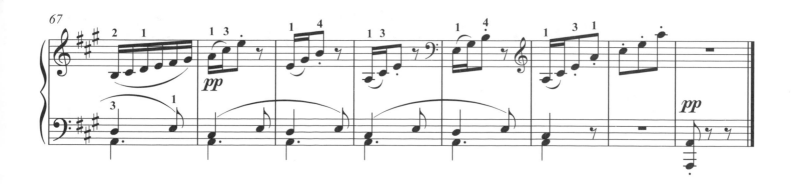

9. An Alexis

No. 59, *from* Pianoforte method

Johann Nepomuk Hummel
(1778 – 1837)

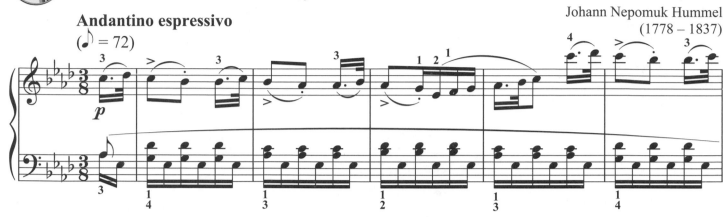

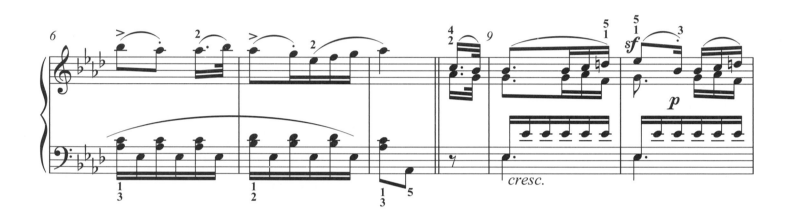

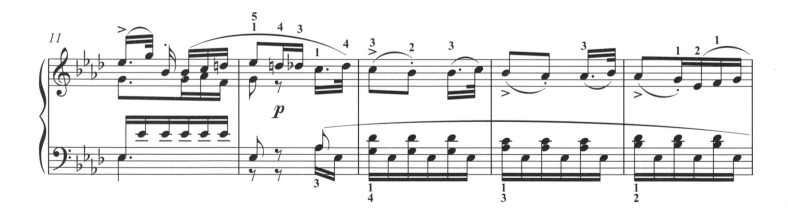

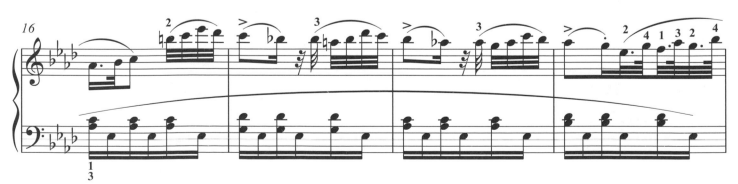

Fingering by the Composer

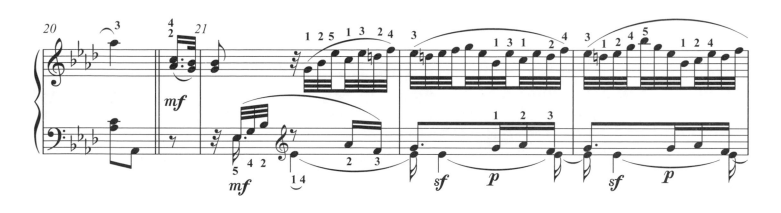

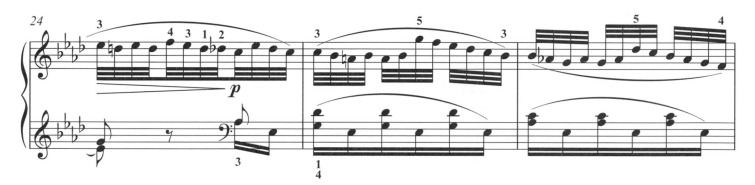

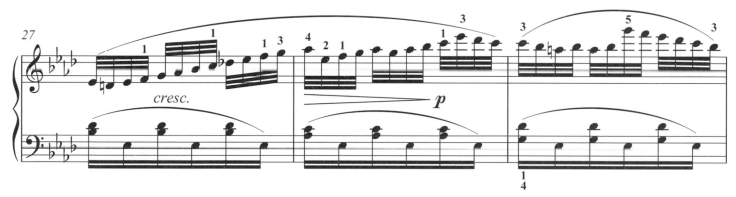

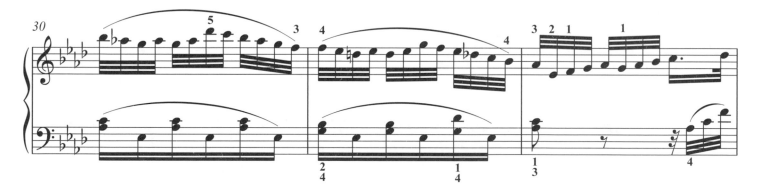

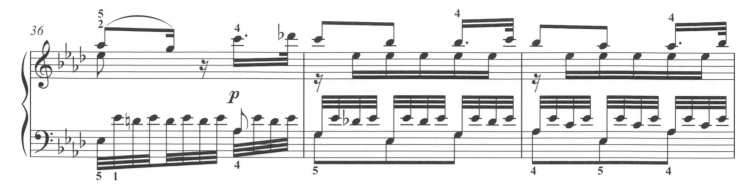

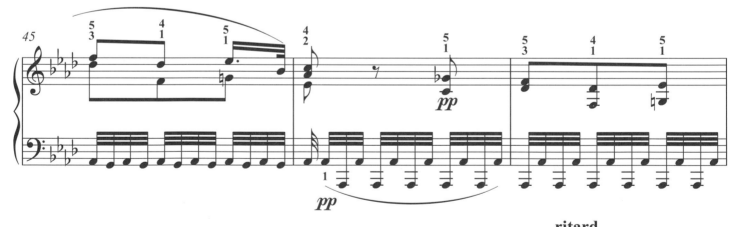

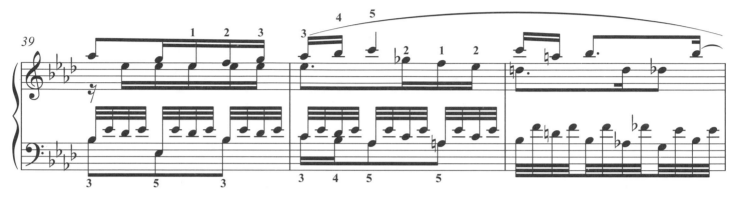

ritard.

10. Adagio

KV 356

Wolfgang Amadeus Mozart
(1756 – 1791)

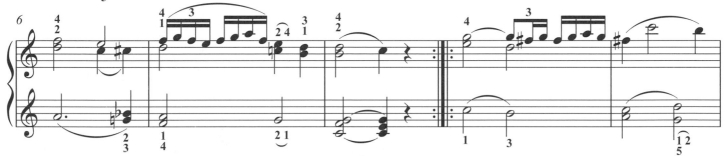

11. Allegretto
D.915

Franz Schubert
(1797 – 1828)

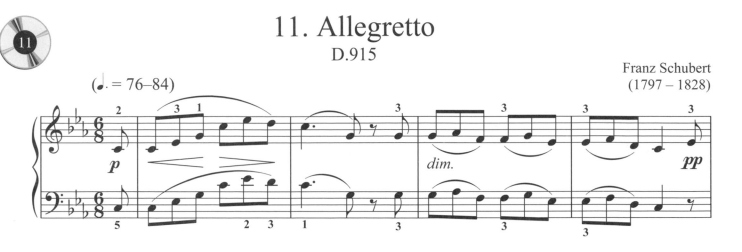

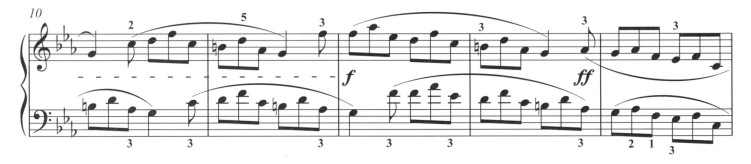

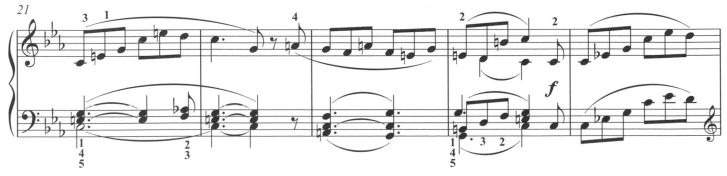

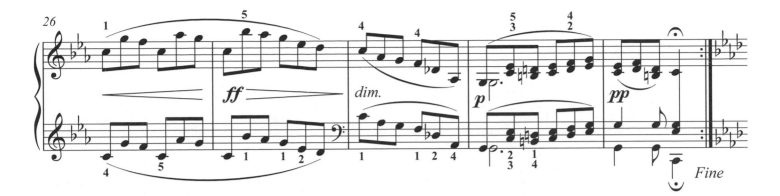

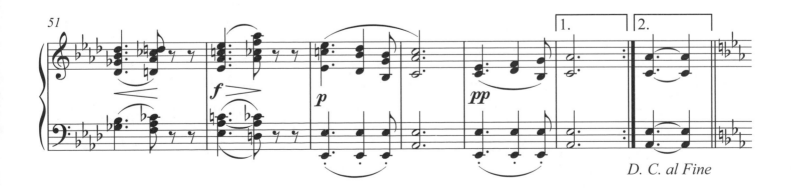

12. Eclogue
Op. 83 No. 1

Gajo sempre l'istesso tempo
(♩. = 88)

Václav Jan Tomášek
(1774 – 1850)

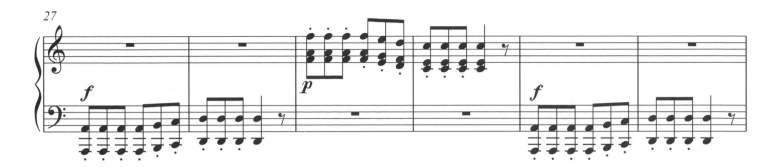

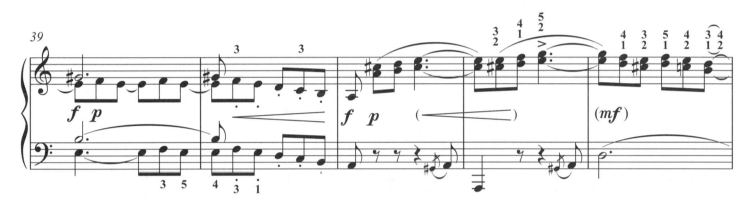

legatissimo e con espress.

D. C. al Fine

13. Andante

D.29

Franz Schubert
(1797 – 1828)

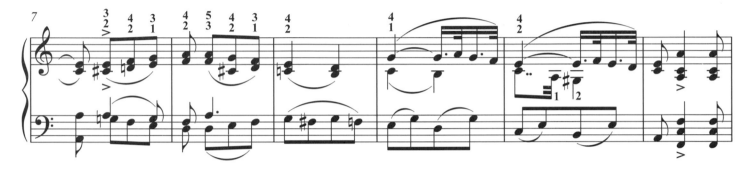

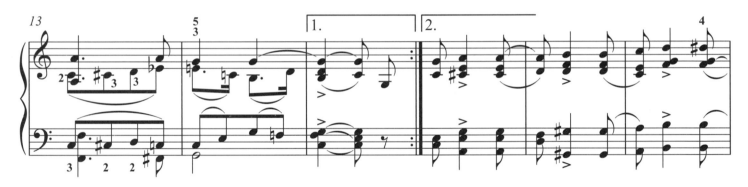

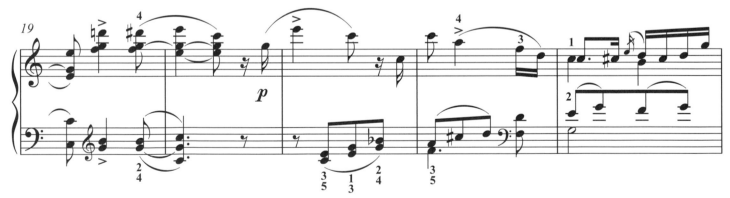

14. Adagio

from Sonata WoO51

Ludvig van Beethoven
(1770 – 1827)

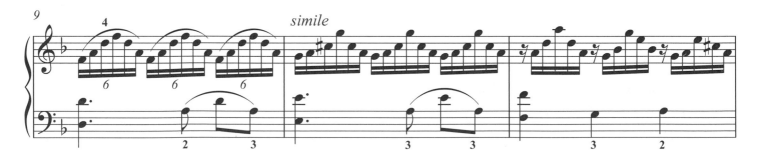

*) Completion from here by Ateş Orga. For the completion by Ferdinand Ries please refer to the Appendix on page 59.

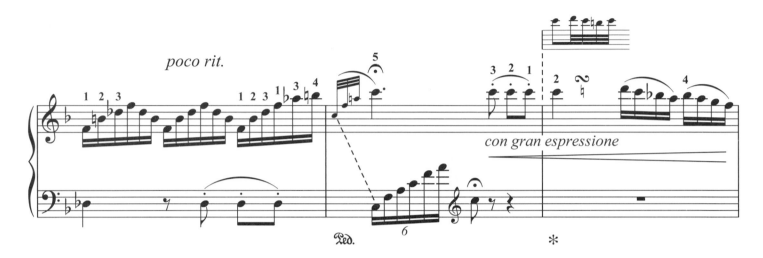

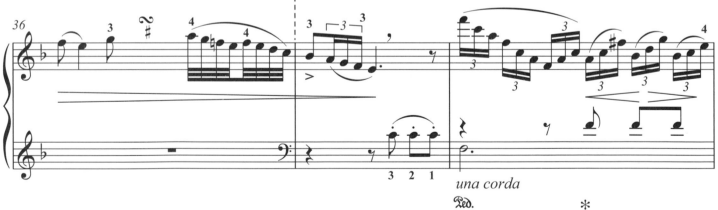

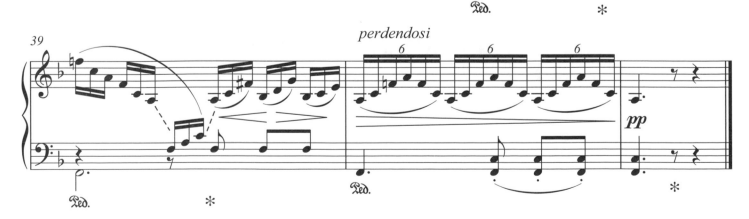

15. Sonata

C.27

Allegro
($\quad$ = 112)

Domenico Cimarosa
(1749 – 1801)

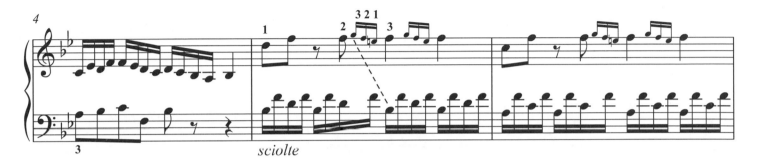

sciolte

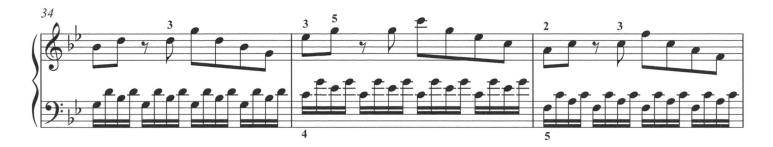

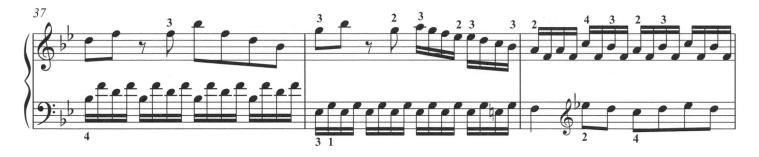

16. Rondo

Op. 18. No. 2

Jan Václav Voříšek
(1791 – 1825)

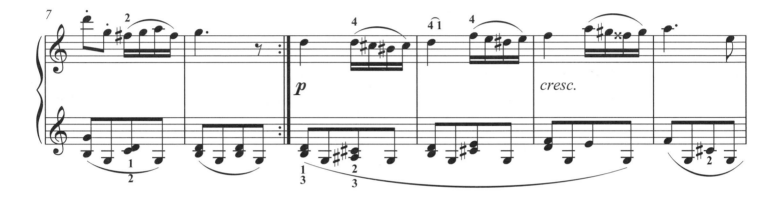

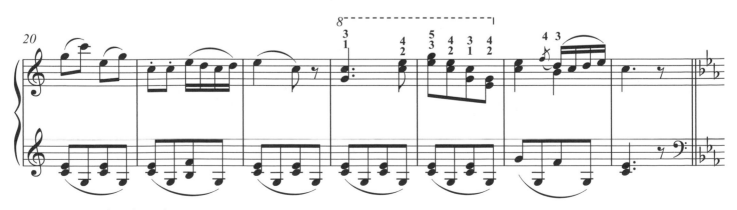

Maggiore

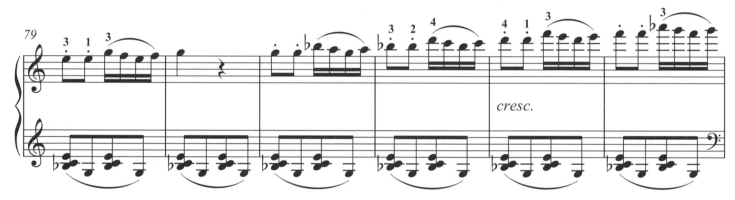

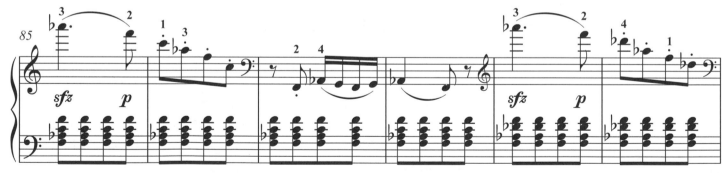

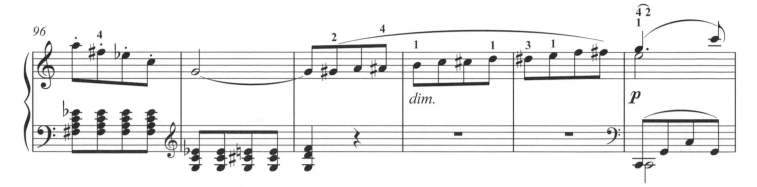

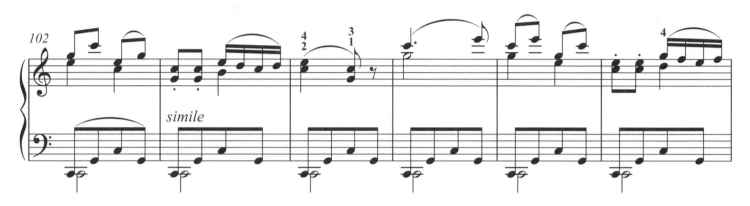

17. Scherzo

D.593 No. 1

Franz Schubert
(1797 – 1828)

Allegretto
(♩ = 124–128)

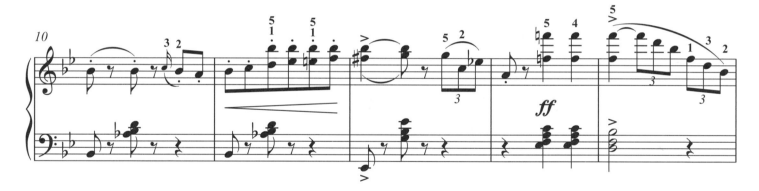

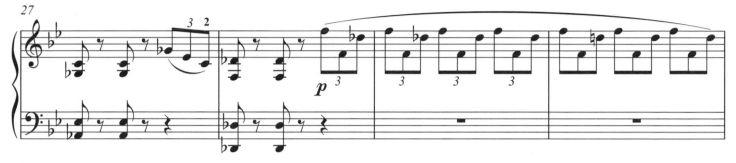

(Fine)

Trio

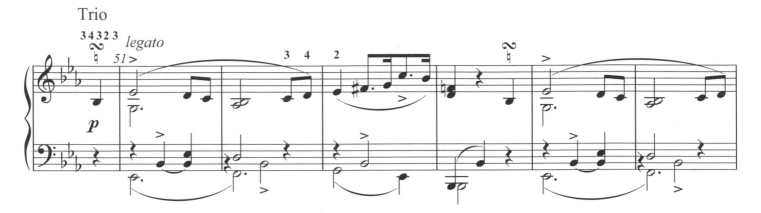

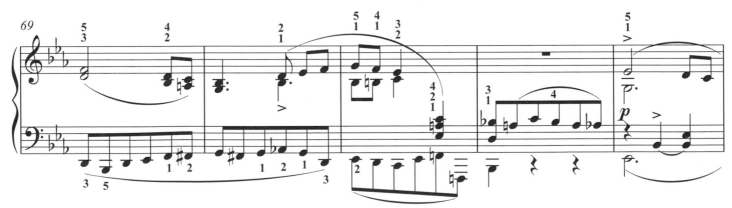

Scherzo D. C.

18. Etude
Op. 161 No. 4

Carl Czerny
(1791 – 1857)

Allego vivo
(♩ = 120–124)

Teaching Notes

One of the interesting challenges of playing music of this period is how we negotiate the difference between the fortepiano of the late 18th century and the piano of today. These differences are quite considerable, but incorporating the knowledge of period instruments while playing modern pianos can only enhance how we respond to the music. For example, the piano in the classical period had lighter keys (and fewer of them), strings that ran parallel to each other as opposed to being cross-strung, leather not felt on the hammers, slighter proportions, no metal frame (wooden instead) and a different action, too. All of this means that we can't recreate a sound as Haydn or Mozart may have heard it, but we can play the modern piano in a way that is respectful of these other musical textures. To achieve that, you might want to use sharply contrasted dynamic differences between *forte* and *piano*, and treat the right pedal as something that enhances the music at specific points, rather than being ever present. The basic sound quality should also be focused more on the treble of the instrument, rather than being bass orientated. Ornamentation too, is important and the CD recording contains the occasional ornament at a cadential point. The use of ornaments is often a matter of personal choice and therefore the best way to think of ornaments is as a subtle enhancing of a melody line.

Ultimately, the concept of historically informed performance practice (being aware of and influenced by an understanding of how music of a different period may have been played) is an excellent basis for experimenting with music, for listening, evaluating and decision-making.

Ludwig van Beethoven (1770–1827)

7. Walzer WoO84

($\downarrow$. = 72)

This piece dates from the last of Beethoven's three distinctive compositional periods; a time when, in his piano music, the composer explored the textures that the extreme registers of the instrument offered. This is particularly evident in the *Trio*, in which the opposing of registers is enhanced by a rhythmic juxtaposition of left and right hands; the left is firmly positioned on the strong beat of the bar whereas the melody in the right hand starts on an upbeat. This contrast is only resolved half way through the *Trio*, with the introduction of *sf* markings in the first beat of the bar. The opening section (bars 1–8) needs a lilting accompaniment figure of the left hand whereas in the subsequent bars (9–16) the composer covers the presence of a waltzing left hand pattern with a distinctive and dynamically varied melody line.

14. Adagio, from Sonata WoO51

($\downarrow$ = 54)

This movement is the second of two that survive of an early piano sonata by Beethoven, now believed to have been written in 1791–2. Whilst the first movement is complete, the composer's manuscript breaks off after the initial 25 bars. At the time of writing, there seem to be two completions of the movement in print, the first by Beethoven's pupil Ferdinand Ries (1830) and the second by Ateş Orga (1975), which is also the version recorded here. For the purpose of comparison, Ries' completion is offered as an appendix in this anthology. The reason for selecting Orga's completion over that of Beethoven's former student is that the composer's contemporaries were united in acknowledging Beethoven's capacity to surprise, whether in performance or composition. Tomášek wrote

that 'I admired his powerful and brilliant playing, but his frequent daring deviations from one motif to another, whereby the organic connection, the gradual development of idea was put aside, did not escape me'.[1] It is this spirit of surprise and extemporisation that shapes, for example, the small cadenza of bars 34–37, making Orga's completion less predictable and an altogether more personal response than Ries' solution.

The choice of tempo should be determined by the demisemiquavers of bar five which need to sound effortless. Having established that tempo, it can then be applied to the opening section of the work.

Domenico Cimarosa (1749–1801)

15. Sonata C.27

($\downarrow$ = 112)

This sonata, like many of Cimarosa's more successful keyboard works, sparkles with light musical textures that lie well under the fingers and are a pleasure to listen to. One of the slight dangers of music such as this, is that the continuous semiquaver texture can easily tempt the player to get faster and faster. So maintaining a controlled tempo and capturing the elegance of the music is arguably the main focus when playing this work. The ornament in bar 5, a turn, should start on the beat which may result in a rhythmic division such as this:

The sonata, which only survives in a copyist's version, has no dynamic markings or musical agogics in the score. All that is given are the notes and the tempo indication, *Allegro*. What at first seems like an unusually bare score soon becomes an excellent opportunity for teachers and students to make decisions of their own. What sort of touch does this piece require? Is there any evidence of terrace dynamics? How should the quavers be articulated? For example, the quavers of bar 29 could be played in the following three different ways:

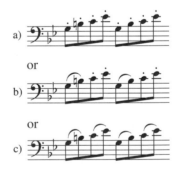

Carl Czerny (1791–1857)

18. Etude Op. 161 No.4

($\downarrow$ =120–124)

As one might expect from one of the most sought-after piano teachers of his time, this etude has a particular technical focus. It is very much concerned with the precision of the semiquavers that shape the piece, but embedded within that idea is the need to retain a flexible wrist at all times. In bars 1–6 this happens within more stationary hand positions, but from bar 7 onwards the flexibility of the wrist supports the finger work in arpeggiated patterns. These

---

1) Sonneck, O. G., *Beethoven. Impressions by his contemporaries*, (New York, Schirmer, 1926), p22

can also be practised as chord progressions, so once a sense of keyboard geography has been developed, the semiquaver practice becomes more comfortable. The fingering given is the composer's, with editorial suggestions in brackets.

Joseph Haydn (1732–1809)

These two works are taken from a collection published under the title of *Différentes petites Pièces faciles et agréables* by the Viennese publisher Ataria in 1786. Whilst there is no composer autograph for the majority of these 10 works, it is reasonable to assume that the pieces, most of which are transcriptions of chamber, symphonic and operatic writing, were either by the composer himself, or at least published in this version with his approval.

1. Allegretto (after Hob. XXVIII:8 [Sinfonia])
(♩. = 76)

There should be a feeling of a comfortable one beat per bar in this dance-like Allegretto. To underline the character of the piece, emphasise the dynamic markings, especially in the *fz* register. Bars 13-27 require some nimble finger work, and a little bit of experimenting with different finger patterns. The fingering given (which is maybe not always the most obvious) is intended to support the articulation of the notes. The triplets in bars 36-37 can be light in touch, almost like a humorous afterthought to the piece.

2. Allegretto (after Hob. XXVIII:8 [Aria])
(♩. = 52)

To develop a sense for the ♩ / ♪ pace of this piece, take the left hand of the opening four bars and play this like a self-contained harmonic pattern. This can help in the establishing of the underlying tempo of the piece. Though not marked as such, the semiquavers in bar 11 repeat the staccato touch of the previous sequence in bars 9-10. The semiquavers at the cadential point in bars 12-13 can then be played legato, in order to emphasise this contrast. The same can apply to the semiquaver scale excerpt from bar 23 onwards.

Johann Nepomuk Hummel (1778–1837)

Both works by Hummel in this anthology are taken from his *Piano Method*, published by Haslinger in Vienna in 1828. The wish to write a piano method had occupied the composer for some time. By 1823 Hummel writes that he 'intends to stay in Weimar, in order to complete his method at last'. By 1826 he reiterates that he has been working on this book for over five years. It has to be acknowledged that Hummel's book of 468 pages is an impressive document. Not only does he address the development of generic musical skills, and of many aspects of pianism, he also reflects on the relationship between teacher and student, and the importance of self-directed learning which he analyses with openness and honesty. Included in this *Method* is a plethora of musical examples, even more finger exercises, and most importantly in the present context, a number of pieces specifically written to develop particular skills.

8. Allegro con brio, No. 45, from *Pianoforte Method*
(♩. = 69)

Hummel's attention to developing both hands in a similar way can be observed by comparing bars 1-4 and 17-20. Bars 38-44 are a small cadenza which leads to the return of the main idea. Bars 53-56 feature a counter melody in the right hand that needs to be balanced with the main motif in the left.

9. An Alexis, No. 59, from *Pianoforte Method*
(♪=72)

Arguably the most musically self-contained of the *60 practice pieces* in Part 1 of Hummel's Piano Method, *An Alexis* is a study in balancing melodic lines with accompanying textures that become gradually more involved. Bars 37-44 consist of four-part writing, in which the tenor and alto lines need to be present without impacting on the clarity of the bass and treble melodies. Practising the notes of each hand separately, but using both hands to do so will help establish an ideal balance between parts, a sound then emulated when playing both parts with one hand, as written.

Leopold Mozart (1719-1787)

4. Allegro moderato [in F]
(♩ = 96)

The main technical challenge of the piece is the synchronising of the tempo of a group of four semiquavers, and the corresponding hand crossing, where applicable. At a moderate tempo, much of this will happen automatically. However, to lay the foundations in slow practice for an eventually much faster performance tempo; imagine each crotchet of the melody line as being a quaver, allowing for the second half of the beat as travelling time. Having achieved this, treat the melody notes as firm semiquavers, allowing for a dotted quaver's worth of hand crossing time. Quite apart from having the time to cross hands, this needs to be a quick movement. To achieve that whilst maintaining the flow of even semiquavers may need a bit of patience. However, having achieved this in principle in bar 1, the same skill can be used throughout the piece, wherever applicable.

The trills can be played as sextuplets, starting on the main note.

Wolfgang Amadeus Mozart (1756-1791)

3. Deutscher Tanz KV 509 No. 3
(♩. = 66–72)

This German dance is the third of a set of six dances, for which Mozart wrote both a piano and an orchestral version, the latter dated 1787. Much of the composer's piano music shows traces of operatic influences, and this dance, too, has different characters within the overall piece. The chords in bars 9–16 hint at a more rounded sound, somewhat more authoritative than the elegant flow of semiquavers in the opening eight bars. The *Minore* is altogether more lyrical, and requires more use of the right pedal to be able to achieve a legato melody line in these double notes. But even then there is a short light-hearted interjection in bars 9–12 of the middle section. However one thinks of a musical narrative, the need for contrast is evident from the different keyboard textures used. One can also make a difference between the semiquavers of the right and left hands. Those found in the latter could be non-legato, whereas semiquavers written in the right hand can be legato.

10. Adagio KV 356
(♩ = 72–76)

This is an interesting piece to play on the modern piano, as there are a number of seemingly contradictory elements to reconcile. Mozart's music, as we understand it today, has a reputation for clarity of sound, yet the instrument this was written for, the *Glasharmonica*, produced exceptionally connected, if not interwoven pitches. Consisting of rotating glass shapes that were touched with slightly dampened fingers, the sounds of the *Glasharmonica* were somewhat ethereal and overlapping, in other words, most unlike what one associates with a Mozartian keyboard texture today. To make the piece work on a modern instrument may require a more extensive use of the right pedal to achieve this level of sonority. The detailed legato fingering for the thirds in bar 3 also highlight the need for a sustained, connected sound.

Michał Kleofas Ogiński (1765–1833)

6. Polonaise [in F]

(♩ = 78)

This short polonaise has appeared in print in several different versions, a most likely result of the composer's ongoing changing of small musical embellishments. Polonaises of the 19th century have increasingly promoted the heroic, extrovert capacity of this dance, whereas Ogiński's piece is a quiet, subtle, almost introspective work. There is no *f* sign in the score, and the opening idea of the piece is marked *dolce e amoroso*. The transition from bar 14 to 15 in the right hand features a repeated *C*. To maintain the fluency in a performance, add the *C* of bar 15 to the turn in bar 14. The given fingering enables the player to do this by changing from the 3rd finger to the thumb. The ornament in bar 23 is best played as a turn that is linked to the two corresponding semiquavers in the left hand.

Franz Schubert (1797–1828)

11. Allegretto D.915

(♩. = 76–84)

The composer dated this piece 26 April 1827 as an entry in a friend's personal album of letters and comments. Historical evidence suggests that it was written spontaneously. If accurate, this offers an insight not only into the type of music Schubert was able to write quickly but it might also come close to how the composer may have improvised at the piano.

The performance direction *Allegretto* needs some explanation. Given the textures of the piece, it is clearly imagined in two comfortable beats per bar. 6/8 here is not the time signature of a fast dance. The staggered entry of two voices in bars 9-13 needs to be clearly audible so that the conversational element between both hands is obvious. Bars 29-30 need careful preparation to achieve a legato sound, based on the collaboration between fingering and pedalling.

13. Andante D.29

(♩ = 46)

Schubert was aged 15 when he wrote this piece, the manuscript of which is dated 9 September 1812. Although written in 2/4, all quaver beats need to have a degree of clarity of sound to enable the melody line of bars 10 and 11 to be crisp and unhurried. Equally, treble and bass lines in bars 24-25 need to be sustained in such a way that alto and tenor lines are audible but not dominant.

17. Scherzo D.593 No.1

(♩ = 124)

To understand the choice of tempo and articulation in this piece, the title Scherzo might need some explanation. Written in 1817, this work is part of a set of two Scherzi D.593. The first seems to be a stand-alone piece, and the trio of the second was re-used in one of Schubert's piano sonatas. From about the 1830s onwards the Scherzo became a virtuoso piano piece, at least as far as the works by Chopin (Scherzi opp.21, 36, 39, 54), Liszt (Scherzo und Marsch) and Brahms (Scherzo op.4) were concerned. Schubert's Scherzi D.593 on the other hand still retain the origin in mood

and spirit of what was formerly a light-hearted, maybe gently humorous character piece.

The fingering in the right hand of the Trio section is guided by the composer's phrase markings. The alto line of bars 59-60 should be taken with the left hand, in keeping with the beginning of the trio. Although not indicated in the score, the joined staccato quavers at the beginning of the Scherzo should be enhanced with a touch of pedal, to enhance the sound of the chord, and to help place emphasis on the first beat of the bar.

Václav Jan Tomášek (1774–1850)

12. Eclogue Op.83 No.1

(♩. = c.88)

Tomášek's *Eclogue* is a good study for working on balancing and voicing chords. Much of the writing is comfortable to play but there is also the odd bar that needs a very carefully considered fingering. For example, bar 15 has some rapid changes of chords. Using the second finger as a pivot on the note G from the second quaver onwards will help the hand positioning (and accuracy) in this bar. Bars 29 to 36 are written for alternating right and left hand, but it is possible to split the chords of bars 31-2 and 35-6 between both hands by taking the lower two notes in the left hand. The notes of the fifth finger of the left hand from bar 48 onwards are harmonic organ points that should be sustained throughout each bar.

Jan Václav Voříšek (1791–1825)

16. Rondo Op.18 No.2

(♩ = 120)

The opening 26 bars of this rondo give little indication of the drama that is to follow once the music changes to c-minor. This central section is thoroughly operatic in its timbral diversity, as is the chordal writing from bar 85 onwards. Given the range of ideas, and the textural way in which these are expressed, it is reasonable to suggest that here is a piece that is equally effective in private study and public performance.

Some the harmonic detail of the left hand from bar 9 onwards ought to be audible, and in juxtaposition to the right hand. There is dynamic contrast, too, not least in the dialogue between bars 30-33 and 33-37. Bars 51-54 are marked *sfz*, meaning a level of attack on each note that still fits into an overall crescendo towards bar 55.

Carl Maria von Weber (1786-1826)

5. Walzer J. App.II/81

(♩. = 56–63)

Weber's Waltz is believed to have been written after the composer improvised the piece at a social gathering in 1825. The repeated notes in bars 1-8 are best played using the editorial fingering given in the score, although not changing fingers when repeating a note does go against some conventions of the time. However, any alternative fingering would seem unduly complicated. To make this fingering work, play the first of two repeated notes lighter that the second.

Biographical Notes

Ludwig van Beethoven (1770–1827)

Beethoven's influence on the direction of music in his time, as well as on the musical developments of subsequent composers, was considerable and multi-layered. His own stylistic development as a composer has resulted in the categorising of his output into three distinct periods: up to about 1802 (early), from 1802–1812 (middle), and from 1812 onwards (late). In terms of Beethoven's piano writing, these periods reflect the classical heritage of his initial phase, the development of his virtuoso keyboard style, and the subsequent structural, as well as technical individuality of his later works.

As a composer, Beethoven excelled in almost all forms of instrumental music, from the string quartet, the piano sonata, to the concerto and the symphony. The spontaneity, strength and emotional impact of his music were nevertheless the result of a meticulously crafted process of composition that is documented in detail in his sketchbooks and autographs. Beethoven was a successful performer as a pianist, though contemporary accounts of his playing differ in their assessment, depending on the focus of the writers. While some praised Beethoven's power and sound projection, others thought his playing to be messy and lacking control. What most sources agree upon though, is the impact Beethoven's playing made upon his listeners.

A piano work that unites both perspectives of his playing is the *Fantasy* for piano op. 77; a work that is largely understood to be the written down version of an improvisation. It contains many Beethovenian features in harmony, melody and texture, and can as such offer a unique insight into the workings of this great musician.

Beethoven's compositional achievements were so considerable that subsequent generations of composers from Schubert to Schumann, Liszt and Brahms hesitated for some time before writing in a genre that Beethoven had previously made his own.

Domenico Cimarosa (1749–1801)

Cimarosa is best remembered as a highly successful composer of operas. After training as a singer, violinist and keyboard player in his native Naples, the growing popularity of his operas enabled him to move from Naples to Venice, then to the Russian court at St. Petersburg where he worked from 1787–1791, and on to Vienna before returning to Naples in 1793. His pro-republican views caused problems for Cimarosa in the politically volatile Italy of the 1790s, and after brief imprisonment in 1799 he returned to Venice where he died in 1801.

Cimarosa's stage works were held in high regard by many of his contemporaries. Haydn is known to have conducted several of Cimarosa's operas, but the reception of his keyboard works is less well documented. Most of the keyboard sonatas are one movement works, and many use binary form. Their transparent style, combined with the structural format, does invite comparisons with Scarlatti's keyboard sonatas, though the melodic material places them firmly in the classical period.

Carl Czerny (1791–1857)

Czerny was, and remains, a significant figure in the development of pianism. Though predominantly remembered for being Beethoven's student and Liszt's teacher, Carl Czerny was an interesting composer in his own right. But the systematic approach in which he developed his own collections of piano exercises was identical with the meticulous way in which he documented his studies with Beethoven, and his early impressions of Liszt. Unsurprisingly, it is in this context that he is mostly remembered.

Czerny's own skills as a composer are possibly best encapsulated in two of his earlier works, the piano sonata op. 7 (performed by Liszt in Paris in 1830) and his highly dramatic symphony in c minor. Aged 16, Czerny decided not to pursue a career as a performer, but to devote himself to teaching instead. This he did, often working for ten hours or more per day until he retired from teaching in 1836.

Czerny left arguably the most comprehensive teaching legacy of any pianist-tutor of his era, as set out in his *Pianoforte-Schule* Op. 500, a work he updated in 1846.

Joseph Haydn (1732–1809)

The evaluation of Haydn's position as a composer has undergone a number of changes over time. A popular perception of Haydn's life is the focus on the relative comfort and stability of his almost 30 year employment by the Esterhazy family in Eisenstadt near Vienna. Despite this comparatively settled existence (at least compared to that of many of his contemporaries, not least Mozart), Haydn's music was published widely post 1780, gaining its composer a growing national and international reputation. Visits to London from 1791 onwards confirmed his musical and economic successes.

However, his early years were very different. After initial training as a chorister and violinist, Haydn, who was not a virtuoso performer, survived by teaching and playing in ad hoc ensembles that provided music for functions. Compositionally, Haydn progressed slowly from being essentially self-taught to gaining the necessary skills. From the mid 1760s onwards Haydn developed a more distinctive musical style.

Haydn's output for piano covers over 60 sonatas, individual pieces, and variations. Though not a virtuoso keyboard performer, Haydn knew exactly how to write effectively for the fortepiano. All of his works lie very well under the fingers (irrespective of their varying degrees of complexity), but it is the element of surprise, both harmonically and in terms of pianistic textures, that gives many of the pieces their particular charm. Overall, Haydn's piano writing is never formulaic and therefore ever so slightly unpredictable.

Johann Nepomuk Hummel (1778–1837)

Hummel was arguably a pivotal figure in his time, both pianistically and compositionally. A pupil of Mozart, Hummel's music always retained its classical roots in terms of its structure and musical detail. Yet as a pianist, and maybe most importantly as an influential piano teacher, Hummel trained many exponents of the first generation of 19th century pianism: Henselt, Hiller and Thalberg all benefitted from Hummel's tuition. Other pianists of the time were also influenced by Hummel. Schumann considered studying with him (he didn't in the end) but Hummel's decorative right hand figurations clearly preoccupied Schumann, as the *Abegg Variations* op. 1 and other early works document. Liszt, too, came into contact with Hummel's music by playing the latter's *Piano Concerti* opp. 85 and 89 early on in his career as a travelling virtuoso. Even Chopin must have been familiar with Hummel's works, as some of his earlier works display some stylistic, occasionally even melodic, similarities.

One of Hummel's outstanding achievements is his piano method of 1828, a 450+ page document that claims to train the student

2) Hummel, J. N., *Anweisung zum Piano-forte spielen*, (Wien: Haslinger, 1828)

'from the first lesson to the most complete training'[2] . Published by Tobias Haslinger in Vienna, it is possibly the 19th century's first comprehensive piano method book that established the technical concepts upon which the virtuoso pianism of that century were based. Hummel's thorough training methodology apart, what makes this method quite remarkable is its author's awareness of and perspective on aspects of pedagogy: student-teacher interaction, motivation, and lesson delivery are amongst the topics that Hummel explores.

Leopold Mozart (1719–1787)

Though mostly remembered today for being the father of W. A. Mozart, Leopold Mozart was a distinguished musician, composer and educator in his own right. After initially studying philosophy, Mozart's musical activities became increasingly important to him. Over a period of twenty years he progressed from a first violinist (sitting number four) to deputy Kapellmeister in the court orchestra of Archbishop Leopold Freiherr von Firmian in Salzburg. He also taught violin and keyboard, leading to the publication of his highly regarded *Violin Method* in 1756. Mozart's ability to write effective music for learners is particularly well documented in the note books for his two children, Nannerl and Wolfgang Amadeus. His compositional output included symphonies, serenades, concerti and keyboard pieces, though many works are now considered lost. Of the pieces that have survived, his dances and smaller works for keyboard are arguably the most frequently performed.

Wolfgang Amadeus Mozart (1756–1791)

Mozart was born into a highly musical environment. His father Leopold worked as an orchestral violinist and educator in Salzburg, and his older sister Nannerl had already shown her ability as a keyboard player. Mozart made rapid progress in his musical studies, so much so that his father decided to take him on a concert tour through Germany to London and Paris. These travels lasted for three and a half years before Mozart returned to Salzburg in 1766. Annual travels to Italy followed from 1769–72, enabling Mozart to come into contact with many other musicians, as indeed he did throughout his life. By the early 1780s Mozart seemed to have settled into life as a freelance musician in all its diversity. Some of his most successful piano concerti date from this period, as do many string quartets, some of which he played alongside their dedicatee, Joseph Haydn. By the end of the decade (and the beginning of the next) Mozart enjoyed considerable success as an opera composer with works such as *Cosi fan tutte* and *Die Zauberflöte*.

The diversity of Mozart's keyboard writing naturally reflects the different periods in the composer's life. Some of the earliest works date from when he was only five, a time when he wrote mostly shorter dances. His mature works include sonatas, variations and individual pieces, many of them written for his own use.

Michał Kleofas Ogiński (1765–1833)

Unlike all other musicians whose works are featured in this volume, Ogiński was not first and foremost a composer or performer. His career as a Polish diplomat enabled him to live and work in cultural centres across Europe where he came into contact with a broad range of musical styles. Born near Warsaw, Ogiński learned to play keyboard instruments (clavichord and fortepiano) and violin, for which one of his teachers is understood to have been the Italian violin virtuoso Viotti. However, it appears that as a composer Ogiński was predominantly, if not entirely, self-taught.

His appointments as a diplomat took Ogiński to, amongst others, Hague in 1789, London in 1790 before moving to Italy in 1794. Two years later he was in Constantinople and by 1802 he was back in Poland where he spent much of his time on musical activities. Appointed Senator of the Grand Duchy of Lithuania in 1811, he withdrew from political life in 1815, moving to Italy where he died in 1833. Nowadays Ogiński is best remembered for writing polonaises for piano, many of which were published in versions for 2 and 4 hands. The piece in this collection is based on a score that the composer wrote as an album leaf in the musical diary of the pianist Maria Szymanowska (1789–1831).

Franz Schubert (1797–1828)

Schubert's initial musical training was provided by his father and brothers who taught him to play the piano, violin and viola. Aged 11 he was a awarded a choral scholarship that enabled him to study with Salieri. By the age of 16, Schubert decided to train as a teacher and a year later started work at his father's school. Aged 17, Schubert had written some of his early masterpieces, *Erlkönig* and *Gretchen am Spinnrade* for voice and piano. In 1816 Schubert relinquished his teaching post, choosing instead to live in the Viennese city centre and concentrating on composition. A period of financial uncertainty followed, but late in 1819 Schubert wrote his first larger scale chamber music masterpiece, the *Trout quintet*. In spring 1821 the success of the *Erlkönig* led to publications of his songs by Diabelli, and thus Schubert experienced a brief period of financial stability. From 1820-23 he was preoccupied by writing operatic music, a less than successful venture, only to turn to writing chamber and symphonic works for the last three years of his life.

Schubert's piano writing is, with few exceptions, never concerned with some of the outwardly technical demands that several of his contemporaries employed. Instead, much of the piano music's demands arise from its preference of musical purpose over any form of pianistic consideration.

Václav Jan Tomášek (1774–1850)

Tomášek was born in Skutec (Bohemia) in 1774. After initial lessons on violin and as a singer, he began to lean the organ. Tomášek's interests were far reaching as his studies of law, mathematics and aesthetics demonstrate. Despite having contact with the composer Kozeluh, Tomášek appears to have acquired most of his musical knowledge through the study of composition treatises, including the writings of Mattheson, Marpurg and Jirnberger. By 1806 Tomášek was appointed music tutor to the family of Count Buquoy in Prague. From the 1820s onwards, he lived as a much respected independent composer and teacher in Prague, where he occupied a central position amongst the city's musical elite. Tomášek was on friendly terms with Haydn and Beethoven, and his work as a teacher produced a lasting legacy. Amongst his pupils were the pianist Alexander Dreyschock (1818- 1869), the musical writer Eduard Hanslick (1825–1904) and the composer Jan Václav Voříšek (1791–1825). Tomášek's most extensive contribution to the piano repertoire are the seven collections of *Eclogues*, predominantly lyrical character pieces, the textures of which anticipated some of Schubert's piano writing and elements of Mendelssohn's *Songs without words*.

Jan Václav Voříšek (1791–1825)

Born in 1791, Voříšek learnt to play violin and organ before attending a grammar school in Prague. From that time onwards he studied music with Václav Jan Tomášek, whose influence on the young composer's development was to be highly significant. By 1813, Voříšek went to Vienna where he soon came into contact with, amongst others, Beethoven, Hummel, Moscheles and Meyerbeer. Voříšek's skills as a pianist were such that when leaving Vienna in 1816, Hummel recommended him to all his piano students as a teacher. Voříšek's impact as a pianist- composer should not be underestimated. His *Impromptus*, published in Vienna in 1822, have rightly been credited with influencing Schubert's works of the same title, written only a few years later. Voříšek's dramatic piano sonata op. 20 is in the then rather unusual key of b flat minor, a choice of key that underlines the composer's ability to capture a sense of musical restlessness that was to shape part of the forthcoming romantic period in music.

Carl Maria von Weber (1786–1826)

Weber's early life is typical of that of many musicians of his time. Receiving his initial musical instruction from his father and several local musicians, Weber's travels around Germany and Austria put him in touch with Michael Haydn (Joseph's brother and a highly respected composer in his own right) and the composer and theorist Georg Joseph Vogler who provided much of the systematic tuition Weber needed. Until 1810, Weber moved from place to place, holding a succession of musical and, in some cases, administrative positions. A court case against Weber and his father, being placed under civil arrest and, ultimately, banned from the area of Würtenberg had a profound effect on Weber. Determined to change his life, he embarked on two years of composing, concertizing and living within his means. Formal appointments as court and/or theatre conductor soon followed; Prague from 1813–16 and Dresden from 1817-1821; periods during which he also continued to travel as a performing musician. Arguably the most significant change in Weber's life occurred due to the extraordinary popularity of his opera *Der Freischütz* (1820), a work that secured him success throughout Germany, as well as internationally.

Weber's piano writing is distinctive, yet also difficult to summarise. It is clearly melodically driven, as is much of his writing, with a particular emphasis on dance forms and dotted rhythmic patterns that underpin his compositional style. As a pianist, Weber is drawn to elaborate and often virtuosic right hand writing; fast moving chord progressions, hand crossing and leaps that go far beyond a hand position. In that sense, Weber's piano writing builds on the fluid scale and arpeggio technique favoured by Hummel, and occupies a half way position between the latter and the pianism demanded by Chopin and Liszt from the 1830s onwards.

Nils Franke

Bibliography

Hinson, Maurice.
Guide to the Pianist's Repertoire.
Bloomington and Indianapolis: Indiana University Press, 2000

MacGrath, Jane.
The Pianist's Guide to Standard Teaching and Performance Literature.
Van Nuys: Alfred Publishing Co., 1995

Prosnitz, Adolf.
Handbuch der Klavierliteratur.
Wien: Doblinger, 1908

Sadie, Stanley (ed.).
Grove Concise Dictionary of Music.
London: MacMillan Publishers, 1988

Sadie, Stanley (ed.)
Grove Dictionary of Music online.
[accessed 04/04/2011]

Wolters, Klaus.
Handbuch der Klavierliteratur zu zwei Händen.
Zürich und Mainz: Atlantis Musikbuch Verlag, 2001

Notes pédagogiques

L'un des enjeux intéressants dans l'interprétation de la musique de cette période réside dans la négociation des différences entre le pianoforte de la fin du 18e siècle et le piano actuel. Ces différences sont assez considérables, mais l'intégration de notre connaissance des instruments d'époque ne peut qu'enrichir la réponse que nous apportons à cette musique lorsque nous la jouons sur un piano moderne. Par exemple, les touches du piano de la période classique étaient plus légères (et moins nombreuses), ses cordes disposées parallèlement et non croisées, ses marteaux recouverts de cuir et non de feutre ; il était de proportions plus réduites, n'avait pas de cadre métallique et possédait également un autre mécanisme. Cela signifie que nous ne pouvons recréer les sonorités telles que Mozart ou Haydn les entendaient, mais nous pouvons jouer du piano moderne en respectant ces textures musicales différentes. Afin d'y parvenir, il faudra user de contrastes dynamiques très différenciés entre *piano* et *forte* et traiter la pédale de droite comme un moyen d'enrichir ponctuellement la musique plutôt que l'utiliser en permanence. Fondamentalement, la qualité sonore devra être axée davantage sur les aigus de l'instrument que sur les graves. L'ornementation est également importante et l'enregistrement figurant sur le CD contient des ornementations occasionnelles dans les passages cadentiels. L'utilisation des ornements est souvent une question de choix personnel. C'est pourquoi, la meilleure façon de l'envisager réside dans l'enrichissement subtil d'une ligne mélodique. Enfin, le concept d'une pratique musicale historiquement éclairée (conscience et influence de la compréhension des pratiques musicales d'une époque différente) constitue une excellente base pour l'expérimentation musicale, l'écoute, l'évaluation et les choix musicaux.

Ludwig van Beethoven (1770–1827)

7. Walzer WoO84
(♩. = 72)
Cette pièce date de la dernière des trois périodes créatrices distinguées dans l'œuvre de Beethoven ; une époque pendant laquelle, dans sa musique pour piano, le compositeur explorait les textures offertes par les registres extrêmes de l'instrument. Cette caractéristique apparaît particulièrement clairement dans le *Trio*, où l'opposition des registres est soulignée par la juxtaposition rythmique de la main gauche et de la main droite ; la main gauche s'appuie fermement sur le temps fort de la mesure tandis que la mélodie, à la main droite, commence sur une levée. Ce contraste ne se résout qu'à mi-parcours du *Trio*, avec l'introduction du *fz* sur le premier temps de chaque mesure. La section d'ouverture (mesures 1–8) nécessite un accompagnement entraînant à la main gauche tandis que dans les mesures suivantes (9–16), le compositeur couvre le motif valsant de la main gauche par une ligne mélodique distinctive et variée du point de vue dynamique.

14. Adagio, from *Sonata WoO51*
(♩ = 54)
Cet *Adagio* est le second des deux seuls mouvements restants d'une sonate pour piano de jeunesse de Beethoven. On estime aujourd'hui que cette dernière fut écrite vers 1791–1792. Alors que le premier mouvement est complet, le manuscrit autographe du second mouvement s'arrête après les 25 premières mesures. À l'heure où nous écrivons, il semble qu'il en existe deux versions imprimées, la première complétée par Ferdinand Ries, un élève de Beethoven, en (1830), et la seconde par Ateş Orga (1975), qui est aussi la version enregistrée ici. La version de Ries figure en appendice à la présente anthologie à fins de comparaison. La raison du choix de la version d'Orga plutôt que de celle de l'ancien élève de Beethoven, repose sur le fait que les contemporains du compositeur s'accordaient tous à lui reconnaître une grande capacité à surprendre, aussi bien en termes d'interprétation que d'écriture. Tomášek écrivait : « J'admire son jeu puissant et brillant, mais ses fréquentes et audacieuses digressions d'un motif à un autre, où le lien organique et le développement progressif de l'idée sont laissés de côté, ne m'ont pas échappé. »[1] C'est cet esprit de surprise et d'improvisation qui caractérise par exemple la petite cadence des mesures 34–37, rendant la version d'Orga moins prévisible et offrant globalement une réponse plus personnelle que la solution proposée par Ries.

Le choix du tempo sera déterminé par les doubles croches de la mesure cinq, qui doivent donner l'impression d'être jouées sans effort. Le tempo ainsi établi pourra ensuite être appliqué aux premières mesures de l'œuvre.

Domenico Cimarosa (1749-1801)

15. Sonata C.27
(♩ = 112)
À l'instar des pièces pour clavier les plus célèbres de Cimarosa, cette sonate étincelle de textures musicales légères venant bien sous les doigts et agréables à écouter. L'un des dangers d'une musique telle que celle-ci réside dans le mouvement continuel de double-croches pouvant facilement entraîner l'interprète à accélérer progressivement. Ainsi, le souci principal dans l'exécution de cette pièce consiste-t–il sans doute à maintenir un tempo contrôlé et à capter l'élégance de la musique. L'ornementation de la mesure 5, un *gruppetto*, devra commencer sur le temps, entraînant la subdivision rythmique suivante :

La partition de la sonate, conservée uniquement dans une version notée par un copiste, ne comporte ni indication dynamique ni indication agogique. Seules y figurent les notes et l'indication générale de tempo, *Allegro*. Ce qui apparaît au début comme une partition inhabituellement dépouillée se transforme rapidement pour les professeurs et leurs élèves en une occasion de prendre leurs propres décisions. Quel esprit insuffler à cette pièce? Comporte-t-elle des indices permettant de déduire une progression dynamique ? Comment articuler les croches? Par exemple, les croches de la mesure 29 pourraient être jouées de trois manières différentes :

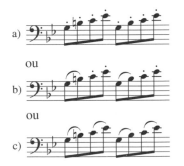

1) Sonneck, O. G., *Beethoven. Impressions by his contemporaries*, (New York, Schirmer, 1926), p.22

Carl Czerny (1791–1857)
18. Etude Op. 161 No.4
(♩ = 120–124)

Comme on peut s'y attendre de la part de l'un des professeurs de piano les plus prisés de son temps, cette étude se concentre sur un aspect technique spécifique. Elle s'attache en effet tout particulièrement à la précision des doubles croches qui caractérisent ce morceau, tout en gardant à l'esprit la nécessité de conserver à tout moment un poignet flexible. Les positions des mains sont relativement stationnaires entre les mesures 1 et 6, mais à partir de la mesure 7, la flexibilité des poignets soutient le travail des doigts dans des motifs arpégés. Ces derniers peuvent aussi être travaillés sous forme de progressions d'accords jusqu'à appropriation de la géographie du clavier, afin que le travail des doubles croches devienne ensuite plus confortable. Les doigtés indiqués sont ceux du compositeur, les suggestions de l'éditeur étant notées entre parenthèses.

Joseph Haydn (1732–1809)

Ces deux pièces sont tirées d'un recueil publié en 1786 par l'éditeur viennois Ataria sous le titre de *Différentes petites Pièces faciles et agréables*. Bien que les manuscrits autographes de la plupart des dix pièces de ce recueil n'aient pas été conservés, il est raisonnable de supposer que celles-ci, dont la plupart sont des transcriptions de pièces de musique de chambre, de musique symphonique et d'opéra, soit sont du compositeur lui-même, soit ont été publiées avec son accord.

1. Allegretto (d'après Hob. XXVIII:8 [Sinfonia])
(♩. = 76)

La sensation confortable d'une pulsation par mesure valorisera cet allegretto au caractère dansant. Pour en souligner le caractère dansant, accentuer les indications dynamiques, en particulier lorsqu'il s'agit du *fz*. Les mesures 13–27 nécessitent une certaine agilité des doigts et l'expérimentation de quelques doigtés différents. Le doigté indiqué (qui n'est pas forcément le plus évident) est destiné à permettre une bonne articulation des notes. Les triolets des mesures 36–37, joués avec une certaine légèreté, apporteront une touche d'humour à la fin de la pièce.

2. Allegretto (d'après Hob. XXVIII:8 [Aria])
(♩. = 52)

Pour développer le sens de la pulsation à la ♩/♪ qui sied à cette pièce, prenez la main gauche des quatre premières mesures et jouez la comme un motif harmonique indépendant. Ce procédé facilitera l'acquisition du tempo de base de la pièce. Bien que cela ne soit pas noté, les doubles croches de la mesure 11 reprennent le *staccato* de la séquence précédente aux mesures 9–10. Les doubles croches cadentielles des mesures 12–13 seront ensuite jouées *legato* afin de souligner ce contraste. La même chose peut s'appliquer aux passages conjoints en doubles croches à partir de la mesure 23.

Johann Nepomuk Hummel (1778–1837)

Les deux pièces de Hummel présentées dans cette anthologie sont tirées de sa méthode de piano publiée à Vienne, chez Haslinger, en 1828. Le projet d'écrire une méthode de piano a occupé le compositeur pendant un certain temps. En 1823, Hummel écrivait qu'il avait « l'intention de rester à Weimar afin de terminer enfin sa méthode ». En 1826, il mentionnait à nouveau qu'il est en train d'y travailler depuis plus de cinq ans. Il faut reconnaître que son ouvrage de 468 pages est un document impressionnant. Il y aborde

non seulement le développement de compétences musicales générales et de nombreux aspects de l'art du piano, mais également la relation maître/élève et l'importance de l'auto-apprentissage, qu'il analyse avec ouverture et honnêteté. Cette méthode regorge d'exemples musicaux, d'exercices pour les doigts et, plus important encore dans le présent contexte, elle contient également un certain nombre de pièces écrites spécifiquement pour le développement de compétences particulières.

8. Allegro con brio, No. 45, tiré de la méthode de pianoforte
(♩. = 69)

Le soin apporté par Hummel à un développement harmonieux des deux mains peut être observé en comparant les mesures 1à 4 et 17à 20. Les mesures 38 à 44 constituent une petite cadence qui conduit au retour de l'idée principale. Les mesures 53 à 56 présentent un contrechant à la main droite qui doit être équilibré par rapport au motif principal joué à la main gauche.

9. An Alexis, No. 59, tiré de la méthode de pianoforte
(♪ = 72)

Sans doute la plus aboutie musicalement des *60 pièces pour l'étude du piano* figurant dans la première partie de la méthode pour piano de Hummel, An Alexis est une étude sur l'équilibre entre la ligne mélodique et des matériaux d'accompagnement de plus en plus complexes. Les mesures 37-44 consistent en une écriture à quatre voix, dans laquelle les parties d'alto et de ténor doivent être présentes sans interférer sur la clarté de la basse et de la mélodie à la voix du dessus. Travailler les notes de chaque main séparément, mais en utilisant les deux mains pour le faire, aidera à établir un équilibre idéal entre les voix. Vous rechercherez ensuite les mêmes sonorités lorsque vous jouerez les deux parties d'une seule main.

Leopold Mozart (1719–1787)
4. Allegro moderato [in F]
(♩ = 96)

Le principal défi technique de cette pièce réside dans la synchronisation du tempo d'un groupe de quatre double croches avec des croisements de mains. À un tempo modéré, cela se fera quasi automatiquement. Cependant, pour poser les fondations en travaillant lentement avant d'accélérer ensuite le tempo d'exécution, imaginez chaque noire de la ligne mélodique au maximum comme une croche, réservant la deuxième moitié du temps au déplacement. Ceci établi, traitez les notes de la mélodie comme des doubles croches que vous jouerez avec fermeté, réservant la durée d'une croche pointée au croisement des mains. Ce déplacement doit être rapide, même si vous ayez suffisamment de temps pour l'exécuter. Y parvenir tout en maintenant un flux régulier de doubles croches peut requérir un peu de patience. Lorsque vous aurez acquis ce principe pour la mesure 1, vous pourrez réutiliser la même compétence tout au long de la pièce, partout où cela est nécessaire.
Les trilles seront joués comme des sextolets, en commençant sur la note haute.

Wolfgang Amadeus Mozart (1756–1791)
3. Deutscher Tanz KV509 No.3
(♩. = 66–72)

Cette danse allemande est la troisième d'un ensemble de six danses dont Mozart a écrit à la fois une version pour piano et une version pour orchestre, cette dernière datée de 1787. La musique pour piano du compositeur dénote pour une grande part l'influence de l'opéra. Cette danse, avec ses nombreux caractères différents, ne fait pas exception. Les accords des mesures 9-16 requièrent un son plus rond, quelque chose imposant davantage l'autorité que le flux élégant de doubles croches des huit premières mesures. La partie intitulée *Minore* est globalement plus lyrique et nécessite un usage plus important de la pédale de droite afin de réaliser une ligne mélodique *legato* dans le passage en tierces. Mais même alors, aux mesures 9–12 de la section centrale, intervient une courte interjection d'humeur légère. Si tout cela évoque une sorte de récit musical, la recherche de contrastes est évidente au vu des différentes textures pianistiques utilisées. Ainsi peut-on marquer une différence entre les doubles croches de la main droite et les matériaux musicaux de la main gauche en utilisant le *legato* pour les unes et pas pour les autres.

10. *Adagio KV 356*
(♩ = 72–76)

Avec ses nombreux éléments a priori contradictoires à concilier, cette pièce est intéressante à jouer sur un piano moderne. La musique de Mozart, telle que nous la comprenons aujourd'hui, possède une réputation de clarté sonore, alors même que l'instrument pour laquelle elle fut écrite, le glass harmonica, produit des sons exceptionnellement liés, voire fondus. Composé de formes de verres en rotation que l'interprète effleure de ses doigts légèrement humidifiés, le glass harmonica produit des sons aériens, parfois imbriqués, en d'autres termes, ne correspondant pas du tout à ce que l'on associe aujourd'hui à la texture de la musique pour piano de Mozart. Pour que la pièce fonctionne sur un instrument moderne, il faut utiliser davantage la pédale de droite afin d'atteindre la même qualité sonore. Le doigté détaillé de legato sur les tierces de la mesure 3 illustre également la nécessité d'un son soutenu et lié.

Michał Kleofas Ogiński (1765-1833)
6. *Polonaise [in F]*
(♩ = 78)

Cette courte polonaise existe en différentes versions imprimées qui témoignent vraisemblablement des petites améliorations apportées continuellement par le compositeur au fil du temps. Au 19e siècle, les polonaises mettaient généralement en avant le caractère héroï-que et extraverti de cette danse, tandis que la pièce d'Ogiński est une pièce calme, subtile, de nature quasi introspective. La partition ne présente aucun *f* et le motif d'ouverture est marqué *dolce e amoroso*. La transition de la mesure 14 à la mesure 15 comporte un *do* répété à la main droite. Afin de maintenir la fluidité de l'exécution, ajoutez le *do* de la mesure 15 au *gruppetto* de la mesure 14. Le doigté indiqué permet à l'interprète de le jouer en effectuant un changement de doigt entre le 3e doigt et le pouce. L'ornement de la mesure 23 bénéficiera d'être exécuté comme un *gruppetto*, en lien avec les deux doubles croches de la main gauche.

Franz Schubert (1797–1828)
11. *Allegretto D.915*
(♩. = 76–84)

Le compositeur a écrit cette pièce dans l'album personnel de lettres et de commentaires de l'un de ses amis en date du 26 avril 1827. Si, comme l'histoire semble l'indiquer, elle a effectivement été composée spontanément, cela donne non seulement un aperçu de ce que Schubert était capable d'écrire en un temps limité, mais aussi de la manière dont le compositeur improvisait au piano.

L'indication *Allegretto* nécessite quelques explications. Compte tenu des textures de la pièce, celle-ci a manifestement été pensée pour deux confortables pulsations par mesure. Ici, le 6/8 ne correspond pas à une danse rapide. L'entrée décalée des deux voix aux mesures 9-13 doit être parfaitement audible afin que l'élément de dialogue entre les deux mains soit apparent. Les mesures 29-30 nécessitent une soigneuse préparation pour parvenir à réaliser un son *legato*, fondé sur l'action conjointe du doigté et de la pédale.

13. *Andante D.29*
(♩ = 46)

Schubert était âgé de 15 ans lorsqu'il écrivit cette pièce, dont le manuscrit est daté du 9 septembre 1812. Bien qu'écrites en 2/4, toutes les croches doivent posséder la même clarté sonore qui permettra à la ligne mélodique des mesures 10 et 11 de résonner avec précision et sans presser. De même, la ligne du dessus et la ligne de basse des mesures 24-25 doit être soutenue de telle sorte que les voix d'alto et de ténor soit audibles mais non dominantes.

17. *Scherzo D.593 No.1*
(♩ = 124–128)

Le titre de *Scherzo* peut nécessiter quelques explications afin d'éclairer le choix du tempo et de l'articulation de cette pièce. Écrite en 1817, cette œuvre fait partie d'un ensemble de deux *Scherzi* D. 593. Le premier semble être une pièce indépendante, tandis que le trio du deuxième a été réutilisé dans une des sonates pour piano de Schubert. À partir des années 1830 environ, le scherzo est devenu une pièce virtuose pour le piano, du moins si l'on considère ceux de Chopin (*Scherzi* opp.21, 36, 39, 54), Liszt (*Scherzo und Marsch*) et Brahms (*Scherzo* op. 4). De leur côté, les *Scherzi* D. 593 de Schubert conservent l'humeur et l'esprit originels de ce qui était précédemment une pièce de caractère légère, parfois teintée d'une touche humoristique.

Les doigtés de la main droite du *Trio* découlent des indications de phrasé du compositeur. La voix d'alto des mesures 59–60 devra être jouée à la main gauche, conformément au début du trio. Bien que cela ne soit pas indiqué dans la partition, les groupes de croches *staccato* du début du scherzo devront être rehaussées d'une touche de pédale afin d'améliorer la sonorité de l'accord et d'accentuer le premier temps de la mesure.

Václav Jan Tomášek (1774–1850)
12. *Eclogue Op.83 No.1*
(♩. = 88)

Cet *Eclogue* de Tomášek est une étude utile pour travailler l'équilibre des accords et leur figuration. L'écriture ne présente la plupart du temps aucune difficulté particulière, mais certains passages nécessitent un doigté très soigneusement étudié. Par exemple, la mesure 15 présente quelques changements d'accords rapides. Utiliser le 2e doigt comme pivot sur le *sol* à partir de la deuxième croche participera au bon positionnement de la main (et à sa précision) dans cette mesure. Les mesures 29 à 36 font alterner main gauche et main droite, mais il est possible de scinder les accords des mesures 31–32 et 35–36 et de confier les deux notes les plus graves à la main gauche. À partir de la mesure 48, les notes du 5e doigt de la main gauche sont des points d'orgue harmoniques qui seront maintenus sur toute la durée des mesures concernées.

Jan Václav Voříšek (1791–1825)
16. Rondo Op.18 No.2
($\quad$ = 120–126)
Les 26 premières mesures de ce rondo donnent peu d'indications
sur le caractère dramatique après le passage en ut mineur. Cette
partie centrale est de nature tout à fait opératique de par la diversité de ses timbres, ainsi que de l'écriture en accords à partir de
la mesure 85. Compte tenu de la variété des idées et de la façon
dont celles-ci s'expriment structurellement, il est raisonnable de
penser que cette pièce fera autant d'effet dans un salon privé qu'en
représentation publique.

À partir de la mesure 9, les détails harmoniques de la main gauche
doivent être audibles, et clairement juxtaposés à la main droite. De
même, les contrastes dynamiques, en particulier dans le dialogue
entre les mesures 30–33 et 33–37 seront respectés. Les mesures
51–54 sont marquées *sfz*, entraînant par conséquent un niveau
d'attaque sur chaque note s'insérant dans le crescendo général
jusqu'à la mesure 55.

Carl Maria von Weber (1786–1826)
5. Walzer J. App.II/81
($\quad$ = 56–63)
Il semble que Weber ait écrit cette valse après l'avoir improvisée
lors d'une réunion mondaine en 1825. Les doigtés proposés par
l'éditeur permettent de réaliser au mieux les notes répétées des
mesures 1–8, bien que le fait de ne pas changer de doigts pour
des notes répétées aille à l'encontre des conventions de l'époque.
Cependant, tout doigté alternatif paraîtrait inutilement compliqué.
Afin que ce doigté fonctionne, alléger la première de deux notes
répétées.

Notes biographiques

Ludwig van Beethoven (1770–1827)

L'influence de Beethoven sur la musique de son temps ainsi que
sur le développement des compositeurs de la génération suivante
a été considérable et multiple. Son propre développement sty-
listique en tant que compositeur débouche sur un classement de
sa production en trois périodes distinctes : jusqu'à environ 1802
(première période), de 1802 à 1812 (période intermédiaire) et à
partir de 1812 (période tardive). En termes d'écriture pianistique,
ces périodes reflètent l'héritage classique de la phase initiale, le
développement de son style virtuose au clavier et l'individualité
structurelle et technique qui en a découlé dans ses œuvres plus
tardives.

En tant que compositeur, Beethoven excellait dans presque toutes
les formes de musique instrumentale, du quatuor à cordes et de la
sonate pour piano au concerto et à la symphonie. La spontanéité,
la force et l'impact émotionnel de sa musique sont cependant le
résultat d'un processus de composition méticuleux, documenté en
détail grâce à ses carnets d'esquisses et ses manuscrits. Beethoven
était un pianiste-interprète reconnu, bien que les témoignages contemporains sur sa façon de jouer diffèrent selon le point de vue de
leur auteur. Tandis que certains louent sa puissance et la projection
du son, d'autres trouvent son jeu brouillon et manquant de contrôle.
Cependant, l'impact du jeu de Beethoven sur ses auditeurs est un
point sur lequel la plupart des sources sont d'accord.

La fantaisie pour piano op. 77 est une œuvre pour piano où ces
deux perspectives de son jeu sont réunies. Souvent considérée
comme la version écrite d'une improvisation, elle contient de

nombreux éléments caractéristiques de l'écriture de Beethoven du
point de vue de l'harmonie, de la mélodie et de la texture, et en
tant que telle, offre un aperçu unique des mécanismes d'écriture
de ce grand musicien.

Les réalisations musicales de Beethoven sont si considérables que
les générations suivantes de compositeurs, de Schubert à Schumann, Liszt et Brahms ont hésité un certain temps avant d'écrire
dans un genre que Beethoven s'était approprié avant eux.

Domenico Cimarosa (1749–1801)

Cimarosa doit sa célébrité actuelle essentiellement à ses opéras.
Après une formation de chant, violon et instruments à clavier
dans sa Naples natale, la popularité grandissante de ses opéras lui
permit de quitter Naples pour Venise, puis pour la cour de Russie
à Saint-Pétersbourg où il travailla de 1787 à 1791. Il se rendit ensuite à Vienne avant de retourner à Naples en 1793. Ses opinions
pro-républicaines lui valurent quelques problèmes dans l'Italie
mouvante des années 1790 et, après un bref emprisonnement en
1799, il retourna à Venise où il mourut en 1801.

Les œuvres scéniques de Cimarosa était tenues en haute estime par
nombre de ses contemporains. On sait que Haydn dirigea plusieurs
de ses opéras, mais la réception de ses œuvres pour instruments
à clavier est moins documentée. La plupart de ses sonates pour
clavier comportent un mouvement unique et utilisent souvent la
forme binaire. Bien que leur matériau mélodique les situe clairement dans la période classique, leur style transparent allié à leur
format structurel invite à les comparer aux sonates pour clavier
de Scarlatti.

Carl Czerny (1791–1857)

Czerny fut et demeure une figure significative du développement
de l'art pianistique. Bien que sa mémoire soit surtout associée à
Beethoven pour avoir été son élève, ainsi qu'à Liszt pour avoir
été son professeur, Carl Czerny est un compositeur intéressant
pour lui-même. Cependant, l'approche systématique qu'il appli-
qua au développement de ses propres recueils d'exercices pour
le piano étant identique à la façon méticuleuse dont il documenta
ses cours avec Beethoven et ses premières impressions de Liszt,
il n'est pas surprenant qu'on se souvienne davantage de lui dans
ce contexte.

Deux œuvres de jeunesse de Czerny, sa sonate pour piano op.
7 (interprétée par Liszt à Paris en 1830) et sa symphonie très
dramatique en *ut* mineur, sont peut-être les meilleurs témoins de
ses dons personnels en tant que compositeur. À l'âge de 16 ans,
il décida de ne pas poursuivre sa carrière de concertiste, mais de
se consacrer en lieu et place à l'enseignement. C'est ce qu'il fit,
travaillant souvent dix heures et plus par jour, jusqu'à sa retraite
en 1836.

Parmi tous les pianistes de son temps, Czerny est sans conteste
celui qui laissa l'héritage pédagogique le plus exhaustif, comme
en témoigne sa *Pianoforte-Schule* op. 500, ouvrage qu'il mit à
jour en 1846.

Joseph Haydn (1732–1809)

L'estimation de la place de Haydn en tant que compositeur a été
soumise à de nombreuses variations avec le temps. La perception
populaire de sa vie se focalise souvent sur le relatif confort et la
stabilité de ses presque 30 ans d'engagement auprès de la famille
Esterhazy à Eisenstadt, près de Vienne. Malgré une existence
effectivement relativement sédentaire (du moins par rapport à
nombre de ses contemporains, et notamment à Mozart), la musique

de Haydn fut largement publiée après 1780, lui permettant ainsi de jouir d'une réputation nationale et internationale croissante. À partir de 1791, ses visites à Londres vinrent confirmer ses succès économiques et musicaux.

Pourtant, ses premières années avaient été très différentes. Après une formation initiale de choriste et de violoniste, Haydn, qui n'était pas un virtuose, survécut en donnant des cours et en intégrant des ensembles jouant de la musique fonctionnelle. Du point de vue de la composition, essentiellement autodidacte, il progressa lentement jusqu'à acquérir les compétences nécessaires qui lui permirent, à partir du milieu des années 1760, de développer un style musical plus caractéristique.

La production pour piano de Haydn comprend plus de 60 sonates, pièces individuelles et variations. Bien que n'étant pas virtuose, il savait exactement comment écrire efficacement pour le pianoforte. Toutes ses œuvres viennent très bien sous les doigts (quel que soit leur degré de complexité), mais c'est l'élément de surprise, à la fois en termes d'harmonie et de texture pianistique, qui donne leur charme particulier à nombre de ses compositions. L'écriture pianistique de Haydn n'obéit jamais à des formules et garde ainsi toujours un caractère légèrement imprévisible.

Johann Nepomuk Hummel (1778–1837)

Hummel fut indubitablement une figure charnière de son époque, tant du point de vue pianistique que de l'écriture. La musique de Hummel, qui fut l'élève de Mozart, conserva toujours ses racines classiques en termes de structure et de détail musical. Cependant, en tant que pianiste, et plus important sans doute, en tant que professeur de piano influent, Hummel forma de nombreux représentants de la première génération du pianisme du 19ᵉ siècle : Henselt, Hiller, Mendelssohn et Thalberg ont tous bénéficié de son enseignement. D'autres pianistes de cette époque ont également subi son influence. Schumann envisagea d'étudier avec lui et si, pour finir, il ne le fit pas, les figurations décoratives de Hummel à la main droite l'occupèrent clairement, comme en témoignent les *Variations Abegg* op. 1 ainsi que d'autres œuvres de jeunesse. Liszt entra lui aussi en contact avec la musique de Hummel en jouant ses concertos pour piano op. 85 et 89 au début de sa carrière de virtuose itinérant. Même Chopin fut sans doute familier de la musique de Hummel, car certaines de ses premières œuvres dénotent des similitudes stylistiques et parfois même mélodiques.

La méthode de piano parue 1828, un document de 450 pages qui prétend mener l'élève « de la première leçon à la formation la plus complète » [2] constitue l'une des réalisations les plus remarquables de Hummel. Publiée à Vienne par Tobias Haslinger (voir morceau nᵒ 10 de la présente anthologie), il s'agit peut-être de la première méthode complète pour piano du 19ᵉ siècle établissant les concepts techniques sur lesquels se fonde l'art pianistique virtuose de cette période. Hormis la méthodologie d'apprentissage approfondie de Hummel, le caractère remarquable de cette méthode réside dans la conscience de son auteur de notions pédagogiques et de ses réflexions s'y rapportant : interaction maître-élève, motivation et déroulement du cours sont parmi les sujets explorés par Hummel.

Léopold Mozart (1719–1787)

Bien que sa réputation actuelle tienne surtout au fait qu'il fut le père de W.A. Mozart, Léopold Mozart fut un musicien distingué, compositeur et pédagogue à part entière. Après avoir commencé par étudier la philosophie, Mozart accorda toujours davantage d'importance à ses activités musicales. En vingt ans, il passa de premier violon (en quatrième position) à vice-maître de chapelle de l'orchestre à la cour de l'archevêque Léopold baron de Firmian, à Salzbourg. Il enseigna également le violon et les claviers, ce qui le mena ainsi en 1756 à la publication d'une méthode de violon très estimée. La capacité de Mozart à écrire de la musique pédagogique est particulièrement bien documentée grâce aux cahiers qu'il écrivit pour Nannerl et Wolfgang Amadeus, ses deux enfants. Sa production inclut de nombreuses symphonies, des sérénades, des concertos et des pièces pour le clavier, dont un grand nombre sont malheureusement considérées comme perdues. Parmi les pièces qui ont survécu, ses danses et petites œuvres pour claviers sont sans conteste les plus fréquemment jouées.

Wolfgang Amadeus Mozart (1756–1791)

Mozart naquit dans un environnement très musical. Son père Léopold était pédagogue et violoniste dans un orchestre à Salzbourg tandis que sa grande sœur, Nannerl, avait déjà révélé ses capacités au piano. Mozart fit des progrès rapides dans ses études musicales, à tel point que son père décida de l'emmener dans une tournée de concerts en l'Allemagne, puis à Londres et Paris. Ces voyages durèrent trois ans et demi avant que Mozart s'installe à Salzbourg en 1766. S'ensuivirent entre 1769 et 1772 des voyages annuels en Italie, qui permirent à Mozart d'entrer en contact avec de nombreux autres musiciens, comme il le fit tout au long de sa vie. Au début des années 1780, il semble que Mozart se soit établit comme musicien indépendant, avec tout ce que cela implique. Certains de ses concertos pour piano les plus célèbres datent de cette période, ainsi que nombre de ses quatuors à cordes dont il interpréta certain avec Joseph Haydn, leur dédicataire. À la fin de cette décennie (et au début de la suivante), Mozart rencontra un succès considérable comme compositeur d'opéra, avec des œuvres comme *Cosi fan tutte* et *La flûte enchantée*.

La diversité de ses œuvres pour piano reflète naturellement les différentes périodes de la vie du compositeur. Certaines parmi les plus précoces ont été écrites alors qu'il était à peine âgé de 5 ans, une époque où il écrivait principalement de courtes danses. Les œuvres de sa maturité incluent sonates, variations et pièces individuelles écrites le plus souvent à son usage personnel.

Michał Kleofas Ogiński (1765–1833)

Contrairement aux autres compositeurs dont les œuvres sont présentées dans ce recueil, Ogiński n'était ni compositeur ni interprète au premier chef. Sa carrière de diplomate polonais lui permit de vivre et de travailler dans différents centres culturels en Europe, où il entra aussi en contact avec une grande variété de styles musicaux différents. Né près de Varsovie, Ogiński apprit à jouer des instruments à clavier (clavicorde et pianoforte) et du violon. Il semble d'ailleurs que l'un de ses professeurs de violon ait été le violoniste virtuose italien Viotti. Pourtant, il paraîtrait qu'il était principalement sinon totalement autodidacte en tant que compositeur. Ses fonctions de diplomate le menèrent notamment à la Haye en 1789 et à Londres en 1790, avant qu'il se rende en Italie en 1794. Deux ans plus tard, il était à Constantinople et en 1802 de retour en Pologne où il occupa une grande partie de son temps à des activités musicales. Nommé sénateur du Grand-Duché de Lituanie en 1811, il se retira de la vie politique en 1815 et partit s'installer en Italie où il mourut en 1833. De nos jours, Ogiński reste dans les mémoires pour ses polonaises pour piano, dont un grand nombre ont été publiées dans des versions pour 2 et 4 mains. La pièce présentée ici se fonde sur une partition que le compositeur écrivit dans le journal musical de Maria

---

2) Hummel, J. N., *Anweisung zum Piano-forte spielen*, (Vienne: Haslinger, 1828)

Franz Schubert (1797–1828)

La formation musicale initiale de Schubert lui a été prodiguée par son père et par ses frères qui lui enseignèrent le piano, le violon et l'alto. À l'âge de 11 ans, il bénéficia d'une bourse d'études qui lui permit de se former auprès de Salieri. Ensuite, à 16 ans, Schubert décida de se former à l'enseignement et commença un an plus tard à travailler dans l'école de son père. À 17 ans, il avait écrit certains de ses premiers chefs-d'œuvre, dont *Le Roi des aulnes Marguerite au rouet*, pour voix et piano. En 1816, Schubert abandonna son poste d'enseignant et choisit de vivre au centre de Vienne et de se consacrer à la composition. S'ensuivit une période d'incertitude financière, mais à la fin de 1819, Schubert écrivit son premier chef-d'œuvre de musique de chambre, son quintette intitulé *La Truite*. Au printemps 1821, le succès du *Roi des aulnes* déboucha sur la publication de ses airs par Diabelli, qui lui permit de connaître une courte période de stabilité financière. De 1820 à 1823, il se lança dans l'écriture de musique d'opéra, une entreprise malheureusement peu fructueuse, pour finalement se tourner vers l'écriture de musique de chambre et de musique symphonique les trois dernières années de sa vie. À quelques rares exceptions près, l'écriture pianistique de Schubert ne se préoccupe pas d'effets techniques tels que le font certains de ses contemporains. Au contraire, toutes les exigences de sa musique proviennent de la prééminence du propos musical sur toute autre forme de considération pianistique.

Václav Jan Tomášek (1774–1850)

Tomášek naquit à Skutec (Bohème) en 1774. Après ses premières leçons de violon et de chant, il commença à s'orienter vers l'orgue. Tomášek avait de nombreux centres d'intérêt comme en témoignent ses études en droit, en mathématiques et en esthétique. Malgré ses contacts avec le compositeur Kozeluh, Tomášek semble avoir acquis la plupart de ses connaissances musicales par l'étude de traités de composition, notamment les écrits de Mattheson, Marpurg et Jirnberger. En 1806, Tomášek fut nommé maître de musique auprès de la famille du comte Buquoy à Prague. Puis, à partir des années 1820, il vécut à Prague où il occupait une position centrale au sein de l'élite musicale de la ville en tant que compositeur indépendant et professeur hautement respecté. Tomášek entretenait des liens d'amitié avec Haydn et Beethoven et a laissé un héritage vivace en tant que professeur. Parmi ses élèves comptent le pianiste Alexander Dreyschock (1818–1869), le critique musical Eduard Hanslick (1825–1904) et le compositeur Jan Václav Voříšek (1791–1825). La contribution la plus importante de Tomášek au répertoire de piano consiste en ses sept recueils d'Eclogues. Ceux-ci sont des pièces de caractère essentiellement lyrique, dont les textures préfigurent certaines compositions de Schubert pour piano ainsi que certains éléments des *Romances sans paroles* de Mendelssohn.

Jan Václav Voříšek (1791–1825)

Né en 1791, Voříšek apprit à jouer du violon et de l'orgue avant de fréquenter un lycée pragois. Dès lors, il étudia la musique avec Václav Jan Tomášek dont l'influence sur le développement du jeune compositeur devait s'avérer significative. Voříšek se rendit à Vienne en 1813, où il entra rapidement en contact notamment avec Beethoven, Hummel, Moscheles et Meyerbeer. Ses talents de pianiste étaient tels qu'au moment de quitter Vienne en 1816, Hummel le recommanda comme professeur à tous ses élèves de piano. L'impact de Voříšek en tant que pianiste et compositeur ne doit pas être sous-estimé. Ses Impromptus publiés à Vienne en 1822 ont été crédités, à juste titre, d'une certaine influence sur ceux de Schubert, composés seulement quelques années plus tard. La dramatique sonate pour piano op. 20 de Voříšek est écrite dans la tonalité alors plutôt inhabituelle de si bémol mineur, un choix de tonalité qui souligne la capacité du compositeur à rendre une certaine agitation musicale qui allait déterminer plus tard une partie du romantisme en musique.

Carl Maria von Weber (1786–1826)

La première partie de la vie de Weber est emblématique de celle de nombreux musiciens de son temps. Son éducation musicale lui fut prodiguée par son père et par plusieurs musiciens locaux. Ses voyages en Allemagne et en Autriche lui permirent ensuite de rencontrer Michael Haydn (frère de Joseph et compositeur très reconnu) ainsi que le compositeur et théoricien Georg Joseph Vogler qui lui dispensa une grande partie de l'enseignement systématique dont il avait besoin. Weber déménagea de ville en ville jusqu'en 1810, occupant successivement différents de postes musicaux, voire dans certains cas, administratifs. Une action en justice contre Weber et son père ainsi que leur arrestation et, pour finir, leur bannissement du land du Wurtemberg, eurent sur lui un profond retentissement. Déterminé à changer de vie, il passa les deux années suivantes à composer, donner des concerts et à vivre à la hauteur de ses moyens. Il fut bientôt engagé en tant que directeur musical à la cour et/ou au théâtre, d'abord à Prague entre 1813 et 1816 puis à Dresde entre 1817 et 1821, périodes au cours desquelles il continua également à voyager en tant qu'interprète. Le changement sans doute le plus important dans la vie de Weber fut provoqué par l'extraordinaire popularité de son opéra, *Der Freischütz* (1820), une œuvre qui assura son succès dans toute l'Allemagne ainsi qu'à l'étranger.

L'écriture pianistique de Weber est caractéristique, mais reste cependant difficile à résumer. Elle est clairement dominée par la mélodie, dans la mesure où elle est souvent homophonique, avec une attirance particulière pour les formes de danses et les motifs rythmiques pointés qui sous-tendent son style de composition. En tant que pianiste, Weber écrit souvent de manière élaborée et virtuose pour la main droite : des progressions d'accords rapides, des croisements de mains et des extensions dépassant largement la position d'une main. En ce sens, l'écriture pour piano de Weber est fondée sur la technique fluide de gammes et d'arpèges également privilégiée par Hummel, mais il occupe une position intermédiaire entre ce dernier et le discours pianistique de Chopin et Liszt à partir des années 1830.

Nils Franke

Bibliographie

Hinson, Maurice.
Guide to the Pianist's Repertoire.
Bloomington and Indianapolis: Indiana University Press, 2000

MacGrath, Jane.
The Pianist's Guide to Standard Teaching and Performance Literature.
Van Nuys: Alfred Publishing Co., 1995

Prosnitz, Adolf.
Handbuch der Klavierliteratur.
Wien: Doblinger, 1908

Sadie, Stanley (ed.).
Grove Concise Dictionary of Music.
London: MacMillan Publishers, 1988

Sadie, Stanley (ed.)
Grove Dictionary of Music online.
[accessed 04/04/2011]

Wolters, Klaus.
Handbuch der Klavierliteratur zu zwei Händen.
Zürich und Mainz: Atlantis Musikbuch Verlag, 2001

Spielhinweise

Eine der interessanten Herausforderungen beim Spielen klassischer Musik ist der Umgang mit dem Unterschied zwischen dem Pianoforte des späten 18. Jahrhunderts und dem heutigen Klavier. Die Unterschiede sind zwar recht groß, doch können eingebrachte Kenntnisse über die damaligen Instrumente unseren Umgang mit der Musik bereichern, auch wenn wir sie auf modernen Instrumenten spielen. So hatte das Klavier der Klassik leichtere (und weniger) Tasten, die Saiten verliefen parallel zueinander, d.h. es gab keine kreuzsaitige Bespannung, die Hämmer waren nicht mit Filz, sondern mit Leder bezogen, es war insgesamt zierlicher, hatte keinen Metallrahmen und eine andere Mechanik. All das bedeutet, dass wir den Klang, den Haydn oder Mozart hörten, nicht reproduzieren können. Wir können das moderne Klavier jedoch so spielen, dass es diesen anderen musikalischen Gegebenheiten gerecht wird. Um dies zu erreichen, sollte man mit starken dynamischen Kontrasten zwischen *forte* und *piano* arbeiten und das rechte Pedal so einsetzen, dass es nur bestimmte Stellen der Musik hervorhebt und nicht allgegenwärtig ist. Die Klangqualität sollte sich grundsätzlich eher an den Höhen als an den Bässen des Instruments orientieren. Verzierungen sind ebenfalls wichtig, und die CD enthält hin und wieder Verzierungen an Stellen, an denen Kadenzen vorkommen. Da die Verwendung von Verzierungen häufig eine Frage des persönlichen Geschmacks ist, betrachtet man Verzierungen am besten als geschickte Bereicherung einer Melodie.

Letztendlich bildet das Konzept der historisch geprägten Spielpraxis (d.h. ein Verständnis dafür, wie Musik in einer anderen Epoche gespielt wurde sowie der Einfluss dessen auf das eigene Spiel) eine hervorragende Grundlage für das Experimentieren mit Musik sowie für die Fähigkeit zuzuhören, zu bewerten und musikalische Entscheidungen zu treffen.

Ludwig van Beethoven (1770–1827)

7. Walzer WoO84
(♩. = 72)

Dieses Stück stammt aus der letzten von Beethovens drei Schaffensphasen – einer Zeit, als der Komponist in seiner Klaviermusik die extremen Register erkundete, die das Instrument bot. Besonders deutlich wird dies im Trio, in dem die gegensätzlichen Register durch eine rhythmische Gegenüberstellung der linken und rechten Hand verdeutlicht werden: Die linke Hand spielt die betonten Taktschläge, während die rechte mit einem Auftakt beginnt. Dieser Kontrast wird erst in der Mitte des Trios durch die Einführung der Anweisung sf auf der Eins aufgelöst. Die Anfangspassage (Takt 1–8) muss mit einer wiegenden Begleitfigur in der linken Hand gespielt werden, während der Komponist den Walzerrhythmus der linken Hand in den nachfolgenden Takten (9–16) mit einer markanten und dynamisch abwechslungsreichen Melodie überdeckt.

14. Adagio, aus der *Sonate WoO51*
(♩ = 54)

Dieser Satz ist der zweite von zwei Sätzen, die aus einer frühen Klaviersonate von Beethoven erhalten sind und vermutlich 1791-92 entstanden. Während der erste Satz vollständig ist, bricht das Manuskript des Komponisten nach den ersten 25 Takten ab. Zurzeit sind zwei vollendete Versionen des Satzes in gedruckter Form erhältlich: Die erste stammt von Beethovens Schüler Ferdinand Ries (1830) und die zweite von Ates Orga (1975). Letztere wurde für die CD-Aufnahme in diesem Buch verwendet. Zu Vergleichs-

zwecken ist Ries' Version im Anhang zu dieser Anthologie enthalten. Der Grund, warum wir Orgas Version den Vorzug gegenüber Beethovens früherem Schüler gegeben haben, ist, dass Beethovens Zeitgenossen geschlossen sein Faible für Überraschungseffekte erkannten, ob beim Spielen oder beim Komponieren. Tomášek schrieb: „Ich bewunderte sein ausdrucksvolles und brillantes Spiel, doch entgingen mir keineswegs seine häufigen gewagten Abschweifungen von einem Motiv zum anderen, bei denen die organische Verbindung, die allmähliche Entwicklung eines Themas, zu kurz kam." („I admired his powerful and brilliant playing, but his frequent daring deviations from one motif to another, whereby the organic connection, the gradual development of idea was put aside, did not escape me").[1] Es ist dieser Sinn für Überraschung und Improvisation, der z. B. die kurze Kadenz in Takt 34-37 ausmacht. Somit ist Orgas Version weniger vorhersehbar und hat insgesamt eine persönlichere Note als Ries' Version.

Das Tempo sollte sich an den Zweiunddreißigsteln in Takt 5 orientieren, die mühelos klingen sollten. Dieses Tempo sollte dann auf die Anfangspassage des Werkes übertragen werden.

Domenico Cimarosa (1749–1801)

15. Sonata C.27
(♩ = 112)

Diese Sonate sprüht wie viele andere erfolgreiche Klavierwerke von Cimarosa vor Leichtigkeit. Sie lässt sich gut spielen und ist eine Freude für die Zuhörer. Eine geringe Gefahr besteht darin, dass die Sechzehntelläufe dazu verleiten können, immer schneller zu werden. Der Schwerpunkt beim Spielen dieses Stückes sollte also auf einem gleich bleibenden Tempo und dem Herausarbeiten der musikalischen Eleganz liegen. Die Verzierung in Takt 5, ein Doppelschlag, sollte auf dem Schlag beginnen, der zu einer solchen rhythmischen Unterteilung führen kann:

Die Partitur der Sonate, die nur als Version eines Kopisten erhalten ist, enthält keine dynamischen oder agogischen Zeichen. Lediglich die Noten und die Tempobezeichnung, *Allegro*, sind angegeben. Was zunächst wie eine ungewöhnlich karge Partitur aussieht, erweist sich schon bald als hervorragende Gelegenheit für Lehrer und Schüler, eigene Entscheidungen zu treffen. Welchen Anschlag erfordert das Stück? Gibt es Anzeichen für Terrassendynamik? Wie sollen die Achtel artikuliert werden? So gibt es z. B. drei verschiedene Möglichkeiten, die Achtel in Takt 29 zu spielen:

---

1) Sonneck, O. G., *Beethoven. Impressions by his contemporaries*, (New York, Schirmer, 1926), S.22

54

Carl Czerny (1791–1857)

18. Etude Op. 161 No.4
(♩ = 120–124)

Wie man es von einem der meistgefragten Klavierlehrer seiner Zeit erwartet, hat diese Etüde einen besonderen technischen Schwerpunkt: Die Sechzehntel, die das Stück prägen, müssen präzise, aber immer auch mit lockerem Handgelenk gespielt werden. In Takt 1-6 werden sie in relativ statischen Handpositionen gespielt, ab Takt 7 wird die Fingerarbeit bei den Arpeggien jedoch durch die Flexibilität des Handgelenks unterstützt. Die Arpeggien können auch als Akkordfolgen geübt werden; es erleichtert das Üben der Sechzehntel, wenn man sich auf der Tastatur erst einmal besser zurechtfindet. Der Fingersatz stammt vom Komponisten, Vorschläge des Herausgebers stehen in Klammern.

Joseph Haydn (1732–1809)

Diese beiden Werke stammen aus einer Sammlung, die 1786 von dem Wiener Verlag Ataria unter dem Titel *Differentes petites Pieces faciles et agreables* veröffentlicht wurden. Da die meisten der zehn Werke nicht als Autograph des Komponisten vorliegen, kann man davon ausgehen, dass die Stücke – hauptsächlich Bearbeitungen von Kammermusikstücken, Sinfonien und Opern – entweder vom Komponisten selbst stammen oder zumindest mit seiner Genehmigung in dieser Version veröffentlicht wurden.

1. Allegretto (nach Hob. XXVIII:8 [Sinfonia])
(♩. = 76)

Dieses tänzelnde Allegretto sollte sich anfühlen, als würde es aus einem Schlag pro Takt bestehen. Um den Charakter des Stückes zur Geltung zu bringen, sollte die Dynamik deutlich zu hören sein, vor allem im *fz*-Bereich. In Takt 13–27 ist geschickte Fingerarbeit gefragt, bei der verschiedene Fingersätze ausprobiert werden. Der angegebene Fingersatz (der vielleicht nicht immer der offensichtlichste ist) soll die Artikulation der Noten unterstützen. Die Triolen in Takt 36–37 können mit leichtem Anschlag gespielt werden, um das Stück zu einem humorvollen Ende zu bringen.

2. Allegretto (nach Hob. XXVIII:8 [Aria])
(♩. = 52)

Um ein Gefühl für das ♩/♪-Schema des Stückes zu bekommen, sollte man die ersten vier Takte mit der linken Hand wie eine in sich geschlossene harmonische Figur spielen. Dies hilft, das Grundtempo des Stückes zu finden. Obwohl sie nicht entsprechend gekennzeichnet sind, werden die Sechzehntel in Takt 11 wie die vorhergehende Passage in Takt 9–10 *staccato* gespielt. Die Sechzehntel der Kadenz in Takt 12–13 können dann legato gespielt werden, um den Kontrast herauszuarbeiten. Dasselbe gilt für die Sechzehnteltonleiterpassage ab Takt 23.

Johann Nepomuk Hummel (1778–1837)

Beide Werke von Hummel in dieser Anthologie stammen aus seiner Klavierschule, die 1828 bei Haslinger in Wien erschien. Der Wunsch, eine Klavierschule zu schreiben, ging dem Komponisten schon lange im Kopf herum. 1823 schreibt Hummel, er „beabsichtige, in Weimar zu bleiben, um endlich die Schule fertigzustellen." 1826 wiederholt er, dass er seit über fünf Jahren an diesem Buch gearbeitet habe. In der Tat ist Hummels Buch mit seinen 468 Seiten ein beeindruckendes Dokument. Er befasst sich nicht nur mit der Entwicklung allgemeiner musikalischer Fähigkeiten und vieler Aspekte des Klavierspiels, sondern macht sich auch Gedanken über die Beziehung zwischen Lehrer und

Schüler sowie die Bedeutung des selbstbestimmten Lernens, das er offen und ehrlich analysiert. Seine Schule enthält eine Fülle an Notenbeispielen, Fingerübungen und – was heute von Bedeutung ist – zahlreiche Stücke, die eigens für die Entwicklung bestimmter Fähigkeiten geschrieben wurden.

8. Allegro con brio, No. 45 aus der Klavierschule
(♩. = 69)

Hummel legte Wert darauf, dass sich beide Hände gleichermaßen entwickeln, was bei einem Vergleich zwischen Takt 1-4 und Takt 17–20 deutlich wird. Die Takte 38–44 bestehen aus einer kleinen Kadenz, die zur Rückkehr des Hauptthemas führt. Die Takte 53-56 enthalten eine Gegenmelodie in der rechten Hand, die mit dem Hauptmotiv der linken Hand ausgeglichen werden muss.

9. An Alexis, No. 59 aus der Klavierschule
(♪ = 72)

An Alexis ist wohl das musikalisch unabhängigste der *60 Übungsstücke* in Teil 1 von Hummels Klavierschule. Hier geht es um das Gleichgewicht zwischen Melodie und Begleitfiguren, die immer komplexer werden. Die Takte 37–44 sind vierstimmig notiert, wobei Tenor- und Altstimme präsent sein müssen, ohne die Klarheit der Bass- und Sopranmelodie zu beeinträchtigen. Ein gutes Gleichgewicht zwischen den Stimmen entsteht, wenn man die Noten jeder Hand gesondert, aber mit beiden Händen übt. Dadurch entsteht in etwa derselbe Klang, wie wenn man beide Stimmen wie notiert mit einer Hand spielt.

Leopold Mozart (1719–1787)

4. Allegro moderato [in F]
(♩ = 96)

Die größte technische Schwierigkeit des Stückes besteht darin, eine Gruppe aus vier Sechzehnteln in gleich bleibendem Tempo zu spielen und dabei zeitweise die Hände zu überkreuzen. In mäßigem Tempo klappt das fast von selbst. Um jedoch den Grundstein für das wesentlich schnellere Spieltempo zu legen, sollte man sich beim langsamen Üben jede Viertel der Melodie höchstens als Achtel vorstellen und die zweite Hälfte des Schlags als Puffer einkalkulieren. Wenn das klappt, kann man die Melodienoten als Sechzehntel spielen und die Dauer einer punktierten Achtel zum Überkreuzen berücksichtigen. Unabhängig davon, ob man Zeit zum Überkreuzen der Hände hat, muss die Bewegung schnell erfolgen. Um dies zusammen mit dem gleichmäßigen Tempo der Sechzehntel zu erreichen, ist etwas Geduld erforderlich. Da man dasselbe im Prinzip jedoch schon in Takt 1 geschafft hat, kann man diese Fähigkeit auch im restlichen Stück anwenden. Die Triller können als Sextolen mit der oberen Note als Anfangston gespielt werden.

Wolfgang Amadeus Mozart (1756–1791)

3. Deutscher Tanz KV509 No.3
(♩. = 66–72)

Dieser deutsche Tanz ist der dritte von sechs Tänzen, für die Mozart sowohl eine Klavier- als auch eine Orchesterversion schrieb – letztere 1787. Mozarts Klaviermusik weist häufig opernhafte Spuren auf, und so hat auch dieser Tanz verschiedene Charaktereigenschaften. Die Akkorde in Takt 9-16 klingen etwas runder und praller als der elegante Sechzehntellauf in den acht Anfangstakten. Die Minore-Variation ist insgesamt gefühlvoller und erfordert einen stärkeren Einsatz des rechten Pedals, um die Melodie mit den Doppelnoten legato zu spielen. Aber selbst dann gibt es einen beschwingten Einwurf in Takt 9–12 des Mittelteils. Was auch immer man von einer musikalischen Erzählung hält: Der Wunsch nach musikalischen Kontrasten wird immer in den vom Komponisten verwendeten unterschiedlichen Texturen deutlich. Man kann auch die Sechzehntel in der rechten Hand anders spielen als die in der linken. Die Sechzehntel der linken Hand können z. B. nicht legato und die der rechten Hand legato gespielt werden.

10. Adagio KV 356
($\downarrow$ = 72–76)

Dies ist ein interessantes Stück für ein modernes Klavier, da viele scheinbar widersprüchliche Elemente vereint werden müssen. Mozarts Musik hat nach unserem heutigen Verständnis immer einen sehr klaren Klang; das Instrument, für das dieses Stück geschrieben wurde, die Glasharmonika, erzeugte jedoch ausgesprochen diffuse, wenn nicht sogar verschwommene Töne. Die Klänge der Glasharmonika mit ihren rotierenden Glasglocken, die mit etwas angefeuchteten Fingern berührt wurden, waren ätherisch und vielschichtig, also völlig anders als das, was heute mit dem typischen Mozartklang assoziiert wird. Damit das Stück auf einem modernen Instrument ebenso voll klingt, kann man verstärkt das rechte Pedal einsetzen. Der ausführliche Legato-Fingersatz für die Terzen in Takt 3 deutet ebenfalls auf den Wunsch nach einem anhaltenden, vielschichtigen Klang hin.

Michał Kleofas Ogiński (1765-1833)
6. Polonaise [in F]
($\downarrow$ = 78)

Diese kurze Polonaise ist in verschiedenen Versionen erschienen – wahrscheinlich als Ergebnis der Veränderungen, die der Komponist permanent an kleinen musikalischen Verzierungen vornahm. Im Gegensatz zu den meisten Polonaisen des 19. Jahrhunderts, die das heroische, extrovertierte Wesen dieses Tanzes ausdrücken, ist Ogińskis Stück ein ruhiges, dezentes, fast beschauliches Werk. Es enthält kein f-Zeichen, und das Anfangsthema trägt die Bezeichnung dolce e amoroso. Der Übergang von Takt 14 zu Takt 15 enthält in der rechten Hand ein C, das wiederholt wird. Um das Stück flüssig zu spielen, sollte man das C aus Takt 15 an den Doppelschlag aus Takt 14 anhängen. Der angegebene Fingersatz sieht dafür einen Wechsel vom 3. Finger zum Daumen vor. Die Verzierung in Takt 23 wird am besten als Doppelschlag gespielt, der mit den zwei Sechzehnteln in der linken Hand verbunden wird.

Franz Schubert (1797–1828)
11. Allegretto D.915
($\downarrow$. = 76–84)

Der Komponist datierte dieses Stück in einem Eintrag in das Privatalbum eines Freundes mit Briefen und Kommentaren auf den 26. April 1827. Historischen Belegen zufolge wurde das Stück spontan geschrieben. Wenn das stimmt, bietet es nicht nur einen Einblick in die Art von Musik, die Schubert auf die Schnelle schreiben konnte, sondern auch in die mögliche Improvisationsweise des Komponisten am Klavier.

Die Spielanweisung Allegretto erfordert eine kurze Erläuterung: In Anbetracht der Struktur des Stückes besteht es eindeutig lediglich aus zwei gefühlten Schlägen pro Takt. 6/8 ist hier also nicht als Taktart eines schnellen Tanzes zu verstehen. Der zeitversetzte Beginn der zwei Stimmen in Takt 9–13 muss deutlich zu hören sein, damit das Gesprächselement zwischen beiden Händen

hervorgehoben wird. Die Takte 29–30 erfordern eine sorgfältige Vorbereitung für die Zusammenarbeit zwischen Fingerstellung und Pedaleinsatz, damit sie legato klingen.

13. Andante D.29
($\downarrow$ = 46)

Schubert war 15 Jahr alt, als er dieses Stück schrieb, dessen Manuskript auf den 9. September 1812 datiert ist. Obwohl es im 2/4-Takt steht, müssen alle Achtel ganz deutlich gespielt werden, damit die Melodie in Takt 10 und 11 klar und locker klingt. Sopran- und Bassstimme müssen in Takt 24-25 so gespielt werden, dass Alt- und Tenorstimme zu hören, aber nicht dominant sind.

17. Scherzo D.593 No.1
($\downarrow$ = 124–128)

Um die Wahl des Tempos und der Artikulation dieses Stückes zu verstehen, sollte der Titel Scherzo kurz erläutert werden. Das Werk wurde 1817 geschrieben und ist eines von zwei Scherzi D.593. Das erste scheint ein eigenständiges Stück zu sein, das Trio des zweiten wurde in einer von Schuberts Klaviersonaten noch einmal verwendet. Ab den 1830er-Jahren wurde das Scherzo zu einem virtuosen Klavierstück, zumindest was die Werke von Chopin (Scherzi op. 21, 36, 39, 54), Liszt (Scherzo und Marsch) und Brahms (Scherzo op. 4) betrifft. Schuberts Scherzi D.593 hingegen entsprechen noch dem Geist des einst fröhlichen, teils humorvollen Charakterstückes.

Der Fingersatz der rechten Hand orientiert sich im Trio an den Phrasierungszeichen des Komponisten. Die Altstimme in Takt 59–60 sollte in Übereinstimmung mit dem Anfang des Trios von der linken Hand übernommen werden. Auch wenn diesbezügliche Angaben fehlen, können die staccato gespielten Achtel zu Beginn des Scherzos durch einen kurzen Pedaleinsatz verstärkt werden. Dadurch klingt der Akkord voller, und die Eins des Taktes erhält eine stärkere Betonung.

Václav Jan Tomášek (1774–1850)
12. Eclogue Op.83 No.1
($\downarrow$. = 88)

Tomášeks Eclogue ist eine gute Akkordvoicing-Übung. Der Großteil des Stückes lässt sich zwar leicht spielen, aber es gibt den einen oder anderen Takt, der einen wohl überlegten Fingersatz erfordert. So enthält z. B. Takt 15 ein paar schnelle Akkordwechsel. Benutzt man ab der zweiten Achtel den zweiten Finger als „Drehpunkt" auf dem G, kann die Hand besser platziert und der Takt genauer gespielt werden. Die Takte 29 bis 36 sind abwechselnd für die rechte und linke Hand geschrieben; man kann die Akkorde in Takt 31-32 und 35-36 aber auch auf beide Hände verteilen, indem man die tieferen Töne mit der linken Hand spielt. Die Töne des fünften Fingers der linken Hand ab Takt 48 sind harmonische Orgelpunkte, die in jedem Takt gehalten werden sollten.

Jan Václav Voríšek (1791–1825)
16. Rondo Op.18 No.2
($\downarrow$ = 120–126)

Die 26 Anfangstakte dieses Rondos geben keinen Hinweis auf das Drama, das nach dem Wechsel zu c-Moll folgt. Der Mittelteil mit seinen vielfältigen Timbres sowie die Akkorde ab Takt 85 muten ausgesprochen opernhaft an. In Anbetracht der zahlreichen Themen und Ausdrucksformen kann man guten Gewissens behaupten, dass das Stück gleichermaßen für private und öffentliche Auftritte geeignet ist.

Ab Takt 9 sollten trotz der Gleichwertigkeit beider Hände einige harmonische Details in der linken Hand zu hören sein. Das Stück enthält auch dynamische Kontraste, nicht zuletzt im Dialog zwischen Takt 30–33 und 33–37. Die Takte 51–54 werden *sfz* gespielt, d. h. dass jeder Ton so angeschlagen wird, dass er immer noch in das *Crescendo* bis zu Takt 55 passt.

Carl Maria von Weber (1786-1826)
5. Walzer J. App.II/81
(♩ = 56–63)
Man nimmt an, dass Webers Walzer geschrieben wurde, nachdem der Komponist das Stück bei einem geselligen Beisammensein 1825 improvisiert hatte. Die Tonwiederholungen in Takt 1-8 spielt man am besten mit dem vom Herausgeber notierten Fingersatz, obgleich es gegen die damaligen Konventionen verstößt, den Finger beim Wiederholen einer Note nicht zu wechseln. Jeder andere Fingersatz wäre jedoch unnötig kompliziert. Damit der Fingersatz funktioniert, sollte die erste der beiden wiederholten Noten leichter angeschlagen werden als die zweite.

Biografische Anmerkungen

Ludwig van Beethoven (1770–1827)
Beethovens Einfluss auf die musikalische Richtung seiner Zeit sowie auf die musikalische Entwicklung nachfolgender Komponisten war beträchtlich und vielschichtig. Seine eigene stilistische Entwicklung als Komponist lässt sich in drei verschiedene Zeitabschnitte einteilen: bis ca. 1802 (erste Schaffensperiode), von 1802 bis 1812 (zweite Schaffensperiode) und ab 1812 (dritte Schaffensperiode). Hinsichtlich Beethovens Klavierkompositionen reflektieren diese Perioden das klassische Erbe seiner Anfangsphase, die Entwicklung seines virtuosen Spielstils und die darauf folgende Individualität seiner späteren Werke in Bezug auf Technik und Aufbau.

Als Komponist zeichnete sich Beethoven in fast allen Formen der Instrumentalmusik aus, von Streichquartetten über Klaviersonaten und Konzerte bis zu Sinfonien. Die Spontaneität, Stärke und emotionale Wirkung seiner Musik waren jedoch das Ergebnis eines akribisch gestalteten Kompositionsprozesses, den er in seinen Skizzenbüchern und Autographen dokumentierte. Beethoven war ein erfolgreicher Pianist, obgleich seine Leistung in zeitgenössischen Berichten je nach Perspektive des Autors unterschiedlich bewertet wurde. Während einige Beethovens kraftvollen Klang lobten, fanden andere sein Spiel chaotisch und unkontrolliert. Die meisten Quellen sind sich jedoch über die Wirkung einig, die Beethoven mit seinem Spiel auf sein Publikum ausübte.

Ein Klavierwerk, das beide Sichtweisen seines Spiels vereint, ist die Fantasie für Klavier op. 77, ein Werk, das weithin als niedergeschriebene Version einer Improvisation angesehen wird. Es enthält viele für Beethoven typische Aspekte hinsichtlich Harmonik, Melodie und Aufbau und bietet daher einen einzigartigen Einblick in das Schaffen des großen Musikers.

Beethovens kompositorische Leistungen waren so beachtlich, dass nachfolgende Komponistengenerationen von Schubert bis Schumann, Liszt und Brahms einige Zeit zögerten, bevor sie in einem Genre komponierten, das Beethoven sich zuvor zu eigen gemacht hatte.

Domenico Cimarosa (1749–1801)
Cimarosa ist als überaus erfolgreicher Opernkomponist bekannt. Nach seiner Ausbildung als Sänger, Violinist und Pianist in seiner Geburtsstadt Neapel konnte er aufgrund der zunehmenden Beliebtheit seiner Opern von Neapel nach Venedig ziehen, ging anschließend an den russischen Hof in Sankt Petersburg, wo er von 1787–1791 arbeitete, und von dort aus nach Wien, bevor er 1793 nach Neapel zurückkehrte. Seine pro-republikanischen Ansichten brachten ihm im politisch unbeständigen Italien der 1790er-Jahre Schwierigkeiten ein, und nach einem kurzen Gefängnisaufenthalt 1799 kehrte er nach Venedig zurück, wo er 1801 starb.

Cimarosas Bühnenwerke wurden von vielen seiner Zeitgenossen überaus hoch geschätzt. So dirigierte z.B. Haydn einige von Cimarosas Opern. Über die Rezeption seiner Klavierwerke ist hingegen weit weniger bekannt. Die meisten seiner Klaviersonaten sind einsätzig, viele sind zweiteilig. Ihre Transparenz in Verbindung mit dem schematischen Aufbau erinnert an Scarlattis Cembalosonaten, obgleich ihre Melodien typisch für die Klassik sind.

Carl Czerny (1791–1857)
Czerny hat maßgeblich zur Entwicklung des Klavierspiels beigetragen. Obwohl er hauptsächlich als Beethovens Schüler und Liszts Lehrer bekannt ist, war Czerny ein interessanter eigenständiger Komponist. Die Systematik, mit der er seine eigenen Sammlungen mit Klavierübungen zusammenstellte, entsprach seiner Art, seinen Unterricht bei Beethoven und seine frühen Eindrücke von Liszt gewissenhaft aufzuzeichnen. Kein Wunder, dass er hauptsächlich in diesem Zusammenhang Erwähnung findet.

Czernys Fähigkeiten als Komponist kommen wahrscheinlich am besten in zweien seiner frühen Werke zum Ausdruck: der Klaviersonate op. 7 (1830 von Liszt in Paris gespielt) und seiner hochdramatischen Sinfonie in c-Moll. Mit 16 Jahren entschied sich Czerny gegen eine Laufbahn als Pianist und für den Lehrerberuf. Als Lehrer arbeitete er häufig zehn Stunden und mehr am Tag, bis er sich 1836 zur Ruhe setzte.

Czerny hinterließ das wohl umfassendste Unterrichtsrepertoire aller Klavierlehrer seiner Zeit, wie an seiner *Pianoforte-Schule* op. 500, einem Werk, das er 1846 aktualisierte, zu sehen ist.

Joseph Haydn (1732–1809)
Die Bewertung von Haydns Stellung als Komponist hat sich im Laufe der Zeit immer wieder verändert. Zahlreiche Berichte konzentrieren sich auf die Sicherheit und Stabilität seiner fast 30-jährigen Anstellung bei der Familie Esterhazy in Eisenstadt bei Wien. Trotz dieses verhältnismäßig beständigen Lebens (zumindest im Vergleich zu vielen seiner Zeitgenossen, nicht zuletzt Mozart) wurde Haydns Musik ab 1780 veröffentlicht und erfreute sich zunehmender Beliebtheit, was dem Komponisten wachsende nationale und internationale Bedeutung einbrachte.

Seine Besuche in London ab 1791 untermauerten seine musikalischen und wirtschaftlichen Erfolge. Seine frühen Jahre sahen jedoch völlig anders aus. Nach seiner Ausbildung als Chorsänger und Violinist hielt sich Haydn, der kein virtuoser Musiker war, mit Unterricht und als Mitglied wechselnder Ensembles, die bei Veranstaltungen musizierten, über Wasser. Als Komponist eignete sich Haydn als Autodidakt nur langsam die notwendigen Fähigkeiten an. Ab Mitte der 1760er-Jahre entwickelteer dann allmählich seinen eigenen Musikstil.

Haydns Klavierwerke umfassen 60 Sonaten, Einzelstücke und Variationen. Obwohl er kein Klaviervirtuose war, wusste er genau, worauf es bei einer Komposition für das Pianoforte ankam. All seine Werke lassen sich sehr gut spielen (ungeachtet ihrer verschiedenen Schwierigkeitsgrade), doch ist das Überraschungsmoment, das sich sowohl in der Harmonik als auch im Aufbau ausdrücken kann, letztendlich für den besonderen Charme vieler Stücke verantwortlich. Haydns Klavierkompositionen sind niemals starr und daher immer unvorhersehbar.

Johann Nepomuk Hummel (1778–1837)

Der Mozartschüler Hummel war zu Lebzeiten eine Schlüsselfigur. Seine Musik blieb sowohl hinsichtlich ihres Aufbaus als auch der musikalischen Details immer ihren klassischen Wurzeln treu. Als Pianist und, was vielleicht am wichtigsten ist, als einflussreicher Klavierlehrer, bildete Hummel jedoch viele Vertreter der ersten Pianistengeneration des 19. Jahrhunderts aus: Henselt, Hiller, Mendelssohn und Thalberg profitierten von Hummels Unterricht. Andere Pianisten jeder Zeit wurden ebenfalls von Hummel beeinflusst. Schumann überlegte, bei ihm Unterricht zu nehmen (tat es jedoch nicht), doch beschäftigte er sich mit Hummels Verzierungen für die rechte Hand, wie die *Abegg Variationen* op. 1 und andere Frühwerke belegen. Auch Liszt kam mit Hummels Musik in Berührung, indem er als junger Klaviervirtuose und Konzertreisender dessen Klavierkonzerte op. 85 und 89 spielte. Selbst Chopin muss Hummels Werke gekannt haben, da einige seiner frühen Stücke stilistische, teilweise sogar melodische Ähnlichkeiten aufweisen. Eine von Hummels herausragenden Leistungen ist seine Klavierschule von 1828, ein über 450 Seiten starkes Werk, das den Anspruch hat, den Schüler „vom ersten Unterricht an bis zur vollständigsten Ausbildung" zu begleiten.[2] Es erschien bei Tobias Haslinger (s. Stück Nr. 10 dieser Anthologie) in Wien und ist wahrscheinlich die erste umfassende Klavierschule des 19. Jahrhunderts, in der die technischen Konzepte enthalten sind, die als Grundlagen für das virtuose Klavierspiel jenes Jahrhunderts dienten. Abgesehen von Hummels gründlicher Unterrichtsmethode zeichnet sich die Klavierschule vor allem durch Hummels pädagogische Erkenntnisse und Betrachtungsweisen aus: Interaktion zwischen Schüler und Lehrer, Motivation sowie die Gestaltung einer Unterrichtsstunde sind einige der Themen, mit denen sich Hummel befasste.

Wolfgang Amadeus Mozart (1756–1791)

Mozart wurde in eine äußerst musikalische Familie hineingeboren. Sein Vater Leopold war Orchesterviolinist und Lehrer in Salzburg, und seine ältere Schwester Nannerl hatte bereits ihre Fähigkeiten als Pianistin unter Beweis gestellt. Mozart machte im Musikunterricht rasche Fortschritte – so rasch, dass sein Vater ihn zu einer Konzertreise durch Deutschland und anschließend nach London und Paris mitnahm, die dreieinhalb Jahre dauerte. Danach ließ sich Mozart 1766 in Salzburg nieder. Von 1769–1772 folgten alljährliche Reisen nach Italien, auf denen Mozart – wie in seinem gesamten Leben – Kontakt zu vielen anderen Musikern knüpfte. Anfang der 1780er-Jahre schien Mozart sich in ein Leben als freischaffender Musiker in all seiner Vielfalt eingefunden zu haben. Einige seiner erfolgreichsten Klavierkonzerte stammen aus dieser Zeit, ebenso viele Streichquartette, von denen er einige an der Seite ihres Widmungsträgers, Joseph Haydn, spielte. Am Ende des Jahrzehnts (und zu Beginn des nächsten) feierte Mozart mit Werken wie *Cosi fan tutte* und *Die Zauberflöte* große Erfolge als Opernkomponist.

Die verschiedenen Lebensabschnitte des Komponisten spiegeln sich in der Vielseitigkeit seiner Klavierkompositionen wider. Einige seiner frühesten Werke entstanden, als Mozart erst fünf Jahre alt war, eine Zeit, in der er hauptsächlich kürzere Tänze schrieb. Zu seinen Werken als Erwachsener zählen Sonaten, Variationen und Einzelstücke – viele davon waren für den Eigengebrauch geschrieben.

Leopold Mozart (1719–1787)

Obwohl er heute hauptsächlich als Vater von W.A. Mozart bekannt ist, war Leopold Mozart ebenfalls ein bedeutender Musiker, Komponist und Pädagoge. Nachdem er zunächst Philosophie studierte, wurden ihm seine musikalischen Aktivitäten immer wichtiger. Über einen Zeitraum von 20 Jahren stieg er vom vierten Violinisten zum Vizekapellmeister im Hoforchester des Erzbischofs Leopold Freiherr von Firmian in Salzburg auf. Darüber hinaus gab er Geigen- und Klavierunterricht und veröffentlichte 1756 seine hoch angesehene Violinschule. Mozarts Fähigkeit, effektive Unterrichtsstücke zu schreiben, ist in den Notenbüchern für seine zwei Kinder, Nannerl und Wolfgang Amadeus, belegt. Seine Kompositionen umfassen zahlreiche Sinfonien, Serenaden, Konzerte und Klavierstücke, obwohl viele Werke als verschollen gelten. Von den noch existierenden Stücken werden die Tänze und kürzeren Klavierstücke am häufigsten gespielt.

Michał Kleofas Ogiński (1765–1833)

Im Gegensatz zu allen anderen Musikern, deren Werke in diesem Band enthalten sind, war Ogiński in erster Linie weder Komponist noch Musiker. Seine Karriere als polnischer Diplomat ermöglichte ihm ein Leben in den kulturellen Zentren in ganz Europa, wo er mit einer Vielzahl musikalischer Strömungen in Berührung kam. Ogiński wurde in der Nähe von Warschau geboren und erlernte Tasteninstrumente (Clavichord und Pianoforte) und Geige, wobei vermutlich der italienische Geigenvirtuose Viotti zu seinen Lehrern zählte. Das Komponieren hatte sich Ogiński jedoch größtenteils, wenn nicht sogar vollständig selbst beigebracht. Seine Termine als Diplomat führten ihn u. a. 1789 nach Den Haag und 1790 nach London, bevor er 1794 nach Italien ging. Zwei Jahre später war er in Konstantinopel, und 1802 kehrte er nach Polen zurück, wo er einen Großteil seiner Zeit der Musik widmete. Nachdem er 1811 zum Senator des Großfürstentums Litauen ernannt wurde, zog er sich 1815 aus dem politischen Leben zurück und ging nach Italien, wo er 1833 starb. Heute ist Ogiński hauptsächlich für seine Polonaisen für Klavier bekannt, von denen viele als zwei- und vierhändige Versionen erschienen. Das Stück in dieser Sammlung basiert auf einer Partitur, die der Komponist als Albumblatt in das musikalische Tagebuch der Pianistin Maria Szymanowska (1789–1831) schrieb.

Franz Schubert (1797–1828)

Schuberts wurde zunächst von seinem Vater und seinen Brüdern unterrichtet, die ihm Klavier, Violine und Viola beibrachten. Im Alter von elf Jahren erhielt er ein Chorstipendium, das ihm eine Ausbildung bei Salieri ermöglichte. Mit 16 Jahren entschied sich Schubert für eine Ausbildung als Lehrer und begann ein Jahr später, in der Schule seines Vaters zu arbeiten. Mit 17 schrieb er bereits einige seiner frühen Meisterwerke für Klavier und Gesang, den *Erlkönig* und *Gretchen am Spinnrade*. 1816 gab Schubert seinen Lehrerposten auf und ging nach Wien, wo er im Stadtzentrum lebte und sich auf das Komponieren konzentrierte. Eine Zeit der finanziellen Unsicherheit folgte, bis er Ende 1819 sein erstes größeres Kammermusikstück, das *Forellenquintett*, schrieb. Im Frühjahr 1821 führte der Erfolg des *Erlkönigs* zur Veröffentli-

---

2) Hummel, J. N., *Anweisung zum Piano-forte spielen*, (Wien: Haslinger, 1828)

chung seiner Lieder durch Diabelli, was ihm eine kurze Zeit der finanziellen Sicherheit einbrachte. Von 1820–23 beschäftigte er sich vorwiegend mit der Komposition von Opernmusik, einem nicht besonders erfolgreichen Unterfangen. In seinen drei letzten Lebensjahren widmete er sich der Komposition von Kammermusik und sinfonischen Werken.

Mit wenigen Ausnahmen legte Schubert in seinen Klavierkompositionen nicht so viel Wert auf die äußerlichen technischen Aspekte, die einige seiner Zeitgenossen anwandten. Stattdessen liegen die Herausforderungen seiner Stücke immer in der Musik selbst und dem Bevorzugen von musikalischer Aussage über rein technischer Darstellung.

Václav Jan Tomášek (1774–1850)

Tomášek wurde 1774 in Skutsch (Böhmen) geboren. Nach anfänglichen Geigen- und Gesangsstunden erlernte er das Orgelspiel. Tomášeks Interessen waren breit gefächert, wie seine Jura-, Mathematik- und Ästhetikstudien zeigen. Obwohl er Kontakt zu dem Komponisten Kozeluh hatte, erwarb sich Tomášek sein musikalisches Wissen anscheinend größtenteils durch das Studium von Abhandlungen über das Komponieren, u. a. Werke von Mattheson, Marpurg und Jirnberger. 1806 wurde Tomášek Musiklehrer der Familie des Grafen Buquoy in Prag. Ab 1820 lebte er als hoch angesehener unabhängiger Komponist und Lehrer in Prag, wo er in der musikalischen Elite der Stadt eine zentrale Stellung einnahm. Tomášek war mit Haydn und Beethoven befreundet und hinterließ als Lehrer ein bedeutendes Erbe. Zu seinen Schülern zählten der Pianist Alexander Dreyschock (1818-1869), der Musikkritiker Eduard Hanslick (1825-1904) sowie der Komponist Jan Václav Voříšek (1791-1825). Tomášeks größter Beitrag zum Klavierrepertoire waren die sieben Sammlungen mit *Eklogen*, überwiegend gefühlvollen Charakterstücken, die einige von Schuberts Klavierstücken sowie Elemente aus Mendelssohns *Lieder ohne Worte* vorwegnahmen.

Jan Václav Voříšek (1791–1825)

Voříšek wurde 1791 geboren und lernte Geige und Orgel, bevor er ein Gymnasium in Prag besuchte. Ab diesem Zeitpunkt war er Schüler von Václav Jan Tomášek, der großen Einfluss auf den jungen Komponisten ausübte. 1813 ging Voříšek nach Wien, wo er u. a. mit Beethoven, Hummel, Moscheles und Meyerbeer in Kontakt kam. Als Pianist hatte Voříšek so überragende Fähigkeiten, dass Hummel ihn bei seiner Abreise aus Wien 1816 all seinen Klavierschülern als Lehrer empfahl. Voříšeks Einfluss als Pianist und Komponist ist nicht zu unterschätzen. Seine *Impromptus*, die 1822 in Wien erschienen, werden zu Recht als Einfluss auf Schuberts gleichnamige Werke, die nur ein paar Jahre später entstanden, gesehen. Voríšeks dramatische Klaviersonate op. 20 steht in der damals eher unüblichen Tonart b-Moll. Mit der Wahl dieser Tonart bewies Voříšek, dass er imstande war, eine musikalische Rastlosigkeit auszudrücken, die später einen Teil der Musik der Romantik ausmachen sollte.

Carl Maria von Weber (1786–1826)

Webers frühe Jahre sind typisch für viele Musiker seiner Zeit. Er erhielt seinen ersten Musikunterricht von seinem Vater und mehreren anderen Musikern. Durch seine Reisen durch Deutschland und Österreich kam Weber in Kontakt mit Michael Haydn (Joseph Haydns Bruder und selbst ein viel beachteter Komponist) sowie dem Komponisten und Musiktheoretiker Georg Joseph Vogler, der Weber den konsequenten Unterricht erteilte, den die-

ser brauchte. Bis 1810 zog Weber häufig um und übte eine Reihe von musikalischen und teilweise auch Verwaltungstätigkeiten aus. Ein Gerichtsverfahren gegen Weber und seinen Vater, im Zuge dessen beide verhaftet wurden und schließlich Württemberg verlassen mussten, hatte tiefgreifende Auswirkungen auf Weber. Entschlossen, sein Leben zu ändern, verbrachte er die nächsten zwei Jahre damit zu komponieren, Konzerte zu geben und nicht über seine Verhältnisse zu leben. Schon bald folgte eine Ernennung zum Hof-und/oder Theaterdirigenten, von 1813 bis 1816 in Prag und von 1817 bis 1821 in Dresden. In dieser Zeit unternahm er außerdem Konzertreisen. Für die wohl bedeutendste Veränderung in Webers Leben war die große Beliebtheit seiner Oper *Der Freischütz* (1820) verantwortlich, ein Werk, das ihm sowohl in Deutschland als auch international Erfolg einbrachte.

Webers Klavierstücke sind zwar sehr charakteristisch, jedoch schwer zu beschreiben. Sie sind eindeutig melodieorientiert wie viele von Webers mehrstimmigen Kompositionen. Ein besonderer Schwerpunkt liegt auf Tanzformen und punktierten Rhythmen, die seinen Musikstil unterstreichen. Als Pianist bevorzugte Weber raffinierte und oft virtuose Passagen für die rechte Hand, schnelle Akkordfolgen, Überkreuzen der Hände und Sprünge, die weit über eine Fünf-Finger-Position hinausgehen. In diesem Sinne beruhen Webers Klavierkompositionen auf der fließenden Tonleiter- und Arpeggiotechnik, die Hummel bevorzugte, nehmen jedoch eine Mittelstellung zwischen Hummel und dem von Chopin und Liszt geforderten Klavierspiel ab 1830 ein.

Bibliografie

Hinson, Maurice.
Guide to the Pianist's Repertoire.
Bloomington and Indianapolis: Indiana University Press, 2000

MacGrath, Jane.
The Pianist's *Guide to Standard Teaching and Performance Literature.*
Van Nuys: Alfred Publishing Co., 1995

Prosnitz, Adolf.
Handbuch der Klavierliteratur.
Wien: Doblinger, 1908

Sadie, Stanley (ed.).
Grove Concise Dictionary of Music.
London: MacMillan Publishers, 1988

Sadie, Stanley (ed.)
Grove Dictionary of Music online.
[accessed 04/04/2011]

Wolters, Klaus.
Handbuch der Klavierliteratur zu zwei Händen.
Zürich und Mainz: Atlantis Musikbuch Verlag, 2001

Appendix / Annexe / Anhang

Ferdinand Ries completion (1830) of the slow movement from Beethoven's *Walzer*, WoO84

CD Track List / Plages du CD / CD-Titelverzeichnis

No.	Title	Composer	Duration
1.	Allegretto (after Hob. XXVIII:8 [Sinfonia]), *from* Différentes petites Pièces faciles et agréables	Joseph Haydn	1:18
2.	Allegretto (after Hob. XXVIII:8 [Aria]), *from* Différentes petites Pièces faciles et agréables	Joseph Haydn	1:12
3.	Deutscher Tanz KV 509 No. 3	Wolfgang Amadeus Mozart	1:15
4.	Allegro moderato [in F]	Leopold Mozart	1:54
5.	Walzer J. App. II/81	Carl Maria von Weber	0:50
6.	Polonaise [in F]	Michał Kleofas Ogiński	1:59
7.	Walzer WoO84	Ludwig van Beethoven	2:02
8.	Allegro con brio, No. 45, *from* Pianoforte method	Johann Nepomuk Hummel	1:13
9.	An Alexis, No.59, *from* Pianoforte method	Johann Nepomuk Hummel	2:22
10.	Adagio KV 356	Wolfgang Amadeus Mozart	3:30
11.	Allegretto D.915	Franz Schubert	4:46
12.	Eclogue Op. 83 No. 1	Václav Jan Tomášek	2:31
13.	Andante D.29	Franz Schubert	4:01
14.	Adagio, *from* Sonata WoO51 (completed Ateş Orga)	Ludwig van Beethoven	2:53
15.	Sonata C.27	Domenico Cimarosa	1:47
16.	Rondo Op. 18 No. 2	Jan Václav Voříšek	2:28
17.	Scherzo D.593 No. 1	Franz Schubert	5:53
18.	Etude Op. 161 No. 4	Carl Czerny	0:49
	Total duration		**42:43**